# I AM A MAN

(Powa ta da Peepas)

## OyamO

APPLAUSE
NEW YORK · LONDON

*Library of Congress Cataloging-in-Publication Data*
OyamO
    I Am A Man / by OyamO
        p.    cm.
    ISBN 1-55783-211-0 (pbk.)
    1. King, Martin Luther, Jr., 1929-1968—Assassination—Drama.    2. Afro-Americans—Civil rights—Drama.    I. Title
PS3565.Y3I2   1995
812' .54—dc20                                                            95-2278
                                                                              CIP

**APPLAUSE BOOKS**

211 West 71st Street                          406 Vale Road
New York, NY 10023              Tonbridge Kent TN9 1XR
Phone (212) 496-7511                  Phone 073 235-7755
Fax: (212) 721-2856                        Fax 073 207-7219

Printed in Canada

*I Am A Man* was commissioned by the Working Theatre, New York City.

Its regional premiere was at the Goodman Theatre, Chicago, IL, May 2, 1994, with the following cast:

| | |
|---|---|
| Bluesman | Olu Dara |
| Martin Luther King | Ron O.J. Parson |
| Reverend Moore | Benny S. Cannon |
| T.O. Jones | Anthony Chisholm |
| Mayor | John Cooke |
| Chief of Police | Steve Pickering |
| Solicitor | Lee R. Sellars |
| Reverend Billings | Tab Baker |
| Senior Negro Councilman | Ellis Foster |
| Alice Mae | Jacqueline Williams |
| Reverend Weatherford | Steve Pickering |
| Miss Secretary | E.J. Murray |
| Black Policeman | Ron O.J. Parson |
| White Policemen | John Cooke, Steve Pickering, Lee R. Sellars |
| Swahili | Clifton T. Williams |
| Brotha Cinnamon | Tab Baker |
| Joshua Solomon | Lee R. Sellars |
| Craig Willins | Johnny Lee Davenport |
| Church Members, Union Members, Voices | The Company |

| | |
|---|---|
| Directed by **Marion McClinton** | Set Design **Scott Bradley** |
| Artistic Director **Robert Falls** | Lighting Design **Pat Dignan** |
| Executive Director **Roche Schulfer** | Dramaturg **Tom Creamer** |
| Costume Design **Caryn Neman** | Musical Supervisor **Olu Dara** |
| Stage Manager **Deya S. Friedman** | Production Stage Manager **T. Paul Lynch** |

# Playwright's Notes

In a sense JONES is the only character in the play. All the others are people who significantly pass through his life, opposing, cajoling, loving, hating, etc., sweeping him along, as it were, through the madly whirling vicissitudes of life. Even the physical staging should reflect his centrality. He should often be center stage, merely turning around to enter the next scene as the lights and images shift.

The BLUESMAN's music sets the tone of the play and is the spiritual environment out of which the story is created. He's always there, though never consciously seen by the other characters in the play. However, his presence can be used playfully. He plays his role without apology for being there, unexplained in the text. He's the blues and its history as the expression of a culture. He is the musical power of Beale Street, the child of field hollers, spirituals and African lament. He is the father of jazz, rock-and-roll, Presley, the Beatles, etc., in a legacy that continues to this moment. But he is definitely not a conventional narrator, and this play is not story theatre with music.

Eleven actors, including Jones, should be a sufficient Ensemble, along with the Bluesman (who sometimes speaks for the other characters, as indicated in the text). The Bluesman should be able to play the harmonica as well as the guitar. If desired, he can be accompanied by three other musicians: keyboard, bass, traps. All the characters talk with "Southern" accents, except WEATHERFORD, SOLOMON and WILLINS. Except where otherwise noted, all characters are black.

The set should essentially consist of projected images, lighting, hangings, and perhaps a few light props and furnishings carried on by actors who unapologetically place them where designated.

THE PACING MUST BE VERY UPTEMPO! Just as fast as the pace at which Jones is spiritually reduced, threatened with loss of power, dignity and pride, in a relatively short time.

**CHARACTERS:**

**BLUESMAN:** Experienced blues vocalist and blues guitar player from whom, in a sense, the entire story emanates, but who is an unobtrusive physical character.

**JONES:** 40, speaks with vocal, gestural and emotional ebullience. Beefy, but average height, very friendly, but also bullheaded about some things. Somewhat vulnerable, a bit fearful and not well educated, quit Memphis Public School in the 8th grade. But he's naturally intelligent—common street sense, a cajoling wit, a generous nature, a lot of heart.

**REV. MOORE:** Late 30's, educated but also "down home" feeling, thinking and, sometimes, speaking. Understands Jones' world and his intentions, but also is aware of the realities of the world of the "others." Is Pentecostal or Church of God in Christ. Colorful dresser, speaks rapidly with lots of gestures, restless manner.

**REV. WEATHERFORD:** Late 30's, white man, a Brit from Canada, patrician looking, quite proper, dapper conservative dressing, but very sincere in his loving nature, a devoted Christian who ministers to a black church. Only slightly naive. A manner that may appear comical to others. Knows how to enjoy a good laugh at himself.

**MAYOR:** A sick man with a mission, but not without a certain dignified dedication, even if to misguided principles, and a gracious civility. Intelligent to the point of arrogance, but a bit insecure about his status and social position. A very stubborn, clever manipulator. A good politician from an old, wealthy Southern family.

**JOSHUA SOLOMON:** White, 50's, tough, N.Y. based labor negotiator who is not averse to swearing and throwing a fit, but who is the ultimate peacekeeper. He's blunt, but always well-meaning. He's thin and full of bantam rooster courage. He knows how to get to a man. He's honest and knows when to stay out of fights. Great agitator and organizer from the old days. Walks with a limp due to childhood polio.

**CRAIG WILLINS:** Black. A brilliant, hardworking labor union troubleshooter with an often nasty disposition. Impatient, pushy, bullying, but sincerely dedicated to the union.

**ALICE MAE JONES:**  Jones' wife. Somewhat ignored by Jones. A mother of five children, weary, lonely, angry. The love she has for her husband has grown fragile over the years.

**MISS SECRETARY:**  Black. Early 30's, First Secretary of the local NAACP, educated, down-to-earth, tries to remain respectful towards people like Jones. Well organized and has good understanding of how to make things happen. Very careful, too careful.

**SENIOR NEGRO COUNCILMAN:**  40's, caught in the middle, but politically astute enough to stay there for the time being, genuinely confused, but wants to be helpful, rather nervous.

**SWAHILI:**  20's, enraged, has grand illusions of the "Black Nation," full of rhetoric and style, but dangerous.

**BROTHA CINNAMON:**  Teenager, a camp follower who wants to be correct, follows orders and repeats slogans. Not really dangerous even in looks. His militant rituals are comical but sincerely practiced.

**POLICE CHIEF:**  White, 50's, an efficient police chief, denigrating towards Jones and Co., would like to "crush" the strike but obeys the Mayor.

**SOLICITOR:**  A closet Southern white Liberal who is exasperated by the system for which he works, honest, angry, rebellious, fed up, practical, compassionate.

**COLLABORATOR:**  A disguised voice and image always in shadows, an undercover informant—impossible to tell whether Collaborator is man, woman, black or white, old or young, a complete mystery.

**REV. BILLINGS:**  30's, an educated bourgeois black preacher from an affluent church, leader in the community.

**TWO COPS:**  One black, one white, young.

**OFFSTAGE VOICES: MLK, WILSON, LAMPLEY, TUCKER, HENDRICKS, VOICES 1,2,3,4,5, AND 6** *at beginning of script.* **VOICES 1,2,3,4** *at very end of script.* **VOICE 2** *at end of script is that of* **KING**.

**TIME:**  January—April, 1968
**PLACE:**  Memphis, Tennessee

# I AM A MAN

## ACT ONE

**PROLOGUE:** *Prominent around the playing areas should be white flats or projection screens onto which the various settings will be projected and strategically placed racks of costumes and necessary props. When the lights are at half, we hear the* VOICE OF MLK.

**MLK'S VOICE:** "And there is, deep down within all of us, an instinct. It's a kind of drum major instinct—a desire to be out front, a desire to lead the parade, a desire to be first. And it is something that runs a whole gamut of life... And the great issue of life is to harness the drum major instinct..."

*The* BLUESMAN *enters alone playing his guitar while the houselights remain up full. The number is an uptempo, dancing blues, a lifejoy blues. (He also can be accompanied by three other musicians, keyboards, bass, traps, if a full combo is desired). The* BLUESMAN *should be able to play the harmonica well. His music remains instrumental until the house is settled at which time the houselights go to black and the* BLUESMAN *begins singing the lyrics in a single spotlight or in a small lighted area near or in the playing space. The song is Muddy Waters' "Garbageman"—From tape "Muddy Waters, Can't Get No Grindin'," MCA Records, Original Chess Records, 1990, actual recording March, 1972. Projected images are of bars along Beale St. and/or of that kind of neighborhood in a typical black urban ghetto setting. Projected on one screen is: JANUARY, 1968. Lights rise on* JONES *who enters alone, salutes the* BLUESMAN, *rhythmically reacts to the music, gets two drinks.* ALICE MAE *enters.* JONES *gives her a drink and seats her in a corner where she sullenly watches him. The* ENSEMBLE *shortly follows. The full lights slowly rise on a jumping Beale Street Bar where off-duty* SANITATION WORKERS *dance popular dances to the "Garbageman" song. Two or more of the* MEN *wear jackets with lettering across their backs that say "MEMPHIS SANITATION DEPT." They are drinking and having a funky ball. There's one or more* WOMEN *present who dance with the men.* JONES *motions to* ALICE *to come dance with him. She shakes her head negatively. He instantly shrugs it off.* SOME MEN *approach him for small loans which he generously gives. The physical gestures of asking and loaning are large. One of the women sexily dances with* JONES *who is a bit of a good humored showoff. The lights crossfade with projections as music fades out. Projections become shifting images of hardworking garbage crews, trucks, garbage. Finally an image of an old style garbage truck is projected. It is a barrel-shaped side loader with a compactor. Images fade to black. In the blackness we hear a thunderstorm raging, the sound of compacting machinery sputtering into motion and the* VOICES OF TWO MEN *screaming for help as they are slowly crushed to death.*

MAN 1:  IT'S GON' HOLD US! IT'S GON' HOLD US!

MAN 2:  NO! KEEP PUSHING! PUSH!

BOTH MEN:  HELP! HELP! HELP!

MAN 1:  IT WON'T STOP!

MAN 2:  KNOCK ON THE SIDE! KNOCK!

*[For a few moments we hear frantic pounding on metal mixed with screams for help.]*

MAN 1:  *[Sobbing, gasping.]* IT AIN'T GON' STOP!

MAN 2:  LAWD GOD HAVE MERCY! HELLLLP!

BOTH MEN:  HELLLLLP!

*[The breath has been crushed from them and all we hear is flesh and bones being smashed, cracked. Then a moment of silence.]*
END OF PROLOGUE

*[As the lights rise slowly, we hear the spiritual hymn "Amazing Grace" being sung by an offstage assemblage of rough male and female voices. They sing it in a "fundamentalist" manner and with great sorrow as if in mourning. Lights rise first on the* BLUESMAN, *accompanying the offstage* VOICES. *Near him are* REV. MOORE *and* JONES. *Projected over their heads is a portrait of the Last Supper. On the flats are projected images of both the interior and exterior of a rather impoverished storefront church in a rundown neighborhood. On one of the flats are projected the words:* STOREFRONT CHURCH, A SUNDAY AFTERNOON, EARLY FEBRUARY, 1968, BEALE STREET, MEMPHIS, TENNESSEE. *As* REV. MOORE *speaks, the* OFFSTAGE VOICES/CONGREGATION *respond verbally to his remarks as during a black fundamentalist church sermon. The* BLUESMAN *speaks the first words of* REV. MOORE's *following speech:]*

**BLUESMAN:** Praise His Name. We've come here this Sunday afternoon to mourn the passing of two good men who died trying to clean up garbage here in Memphis.

**MOORE:** No words will bring those men back to their families, but we can remember that Jesus was a garbage collector too. Praise His Name! He went about the world trying to clean up garbage. People's lives were full of garbage, still are, all kinds of garbage: hatred, spite, envy, vanity, violence, despair. They fight and kill each other in wars all over the world for reasons so old they can't even remember them. Jesus tried His best to destroy the garbage, but, like our dearly departed, He also lost His life. But all of us are better off for it. Praise His Name. I bring my words

VOICE 4:  Dues kinda heavy what we gittin' in return.

JONES:  Fo' dollas? Fo' dollas a munt! Union git us mo' pay, but union need support. Now, you kin argue dat point or you kin move on. Ya'll cain't have no union lessen da union kin collect dues. Got ta hep ourselves. *[Mildly condescending.]* Dat's order, propa order. Sometimes ya'll don't hear me. It break down to dis: You don't do it wit propa order, you cain't do it. I cain't put it more simple. Okay? Look, I put it this way: What ya'll wanna do?

VOICE 1:  I say again strike!

JONES:  And what about the Mayor's '66 injunction against a strike? It's still in force far as I know.

VOICE 1:  What about it? Das yo' job to deal wit dat.

JONES:  And what about support? We stop takin' garbage, everybody upset. We ain't got a hunded dollas in the treasury. You cain't even talk to a lawyer on the phone for less than a hunded dollas. We cain't affo'd no kinda bills ta pay.

VOICE 2:  Why we got to pay somebody else so we kin strike?

VOICE 3:  Cain't we just vote on it. There's 800 men here. Day can speak fah dayself. I move we strike.

VOICE 4:  I second da motion.

JONES:  It's moved and seconded that we strike. Any moe discussion? *[Silence.]* Alright, let me say one thing and den we votes. Callin' a strike on 'r own ain't no small thing. If ya want it ta work, ya'll got ta take holt and push together. People can't be fallin' off when it's time ta move. I been here since the beginnin' and ya'll know dat I ain't never stop fighting fah yaw. But now we gon' hafta fight together. Ya'll ready fah da question?

UNISON:  Question!

JONES:  All those in favor say Aye!

UNISON:  AYE!

JONES:  All those oppose?

*[Silence.]*

JONES:  Da motion carry; Mayor got him a strike.

*[Cheers.]*

Alright, I pledge half my paycheck to the strike fund every munt. And when ya'll pick up ya las' checks on Friday, I'm looking for every man ta put foe dollas in the fund. Is dat clear? On nex' Monday we strike. If 'r demands ain't satisfy, we gon' have every buzzard in five hunded miles comin' ta eat in Memphis 'cause it stink so bad.

*[BLUESMAN picks up on "Every Buzzard" and sings those words blues fashion as Lights and Images shift to a large meeting room in city hall. Suspended above the heads of FOUR MEN meeting is a huge replica of the Memphis City Seal. THE MAYOR, CHIEF OF POLICE, and TOWN SOLICITOR are present. In the shadows appears a figure whose face and body are blotted out. From the clothes or whatever else may be visible it is impossible to tell whether the COLLABORATOR is a man or a woman, black or white. When the COLLABORATOR speaks, it's voice is distorted. The others speak and refer to the COLLABORATOR. The COLLABORATOR can hear but not see the others.]*

MAYOR:  So, essentially we have a wildcat strike.

COLLABORATOR:  Yep. That's about it.

BLUESMAN:  That Jones is such an ignorant man or maybe he's just forgetful.

MAYOR:  Back in '66 we settled all the grievances just by sitting down and talking. This whole thing could be solved if he just came in like a man and talked to me.

COLLABORATOR:  That's just what he intends to do.

MAYOR:  I see. So, is there anything else the Board members and I should be made aware of?

COLLABORATOR:  There is some gossip about T.O. Jones separating from his wife or such.

MAYOR:  Well, that's irrelevant, but good to know. If he can't keep a family together, how does he expect to keep that so-called union together? Chief, you can dismiss your agent, so we can begin our meeting.

CHIEF:  I'll contact you in a few days. You are dismissed.

MAYOR:  Gentlemen, let me make clear that I first conferred with the senior Negro councilman before convening this Advisory Board meeting, and for the record let it be noted that I personally solicited his advice and help. Do I make myself clear?

UNISON:  Quite clear, Mr. Mayor.

SOLICITOR:  *[A bit tense.]* But he should be informed about our deliberations. He is a member of this Advisory Board.

MAYOR:  Duly noted. Now, just in case we can't prevent this so-called strike, I've asked you all to come up with contingency plans. Chief?

CHIEF:  Well, we've been watching 'em closely. Not too much has changed. They still drink on Beale St. and sing the blues, fight a lot, especially on Saturday night. I expect they'll fuss and fume for a day or two and then go back to work. I should  have enough squad cars on hand to escort the garbage trucks and protect  the garages if necessary. I don't expect any mass action here like in other cities, but I'm ready for that too.

MAYOR:  The Sanitation Commissioner feels he can convince at least a hundred sanitation workers to remain at their jobs, and he'll hire another hundred. He plans to have once a week collections within days. Mr. Solicitor?

**SOLICITOR:** *[Weary resignation.]* The 1966 Injunction remains in force, but it's irrelevant to any union worth its salt. Strikes by municipal and state employees are illegal in Tennessee, but International AFCSME is out to challenge that law, even it means jails and fines. A strike is inevitable unless we settle immediately.

**MAYOR:** *[A bit sharply.]* Which is why I look forward to my meeting with Jones.

*[Lights and Images shift to a "bar" on Beale St. where T.O. JONES, the* SENIOR NEGRO COUNCILMAN *and* REV. BILLINGS, *a black minister, sit at a table. The projected images are of Beale St. and its joints circa 1968. The BLUES-MAN sings a medium tempo blues and accompanies himself on guitar. T.O. rocks with the beat obviously enjoying himself. We hear the recorded sounds of* OTHERS *carousing, loudly enjoying the music. A* LONE WOMAN *dances drunkenly, sadly, but seductively. BILLINGS is quite visibly upset being there. When the music fades to silence,* JONES *speaks.]*

**JONES:** Bartender, another beer for the Councilman and a coke for the Rev.

**BLUESMAN:** Do you have to tell everyone I'm a minister?

**JONES:** You is a minister.

**BILLINGS:** I know what I "is." I don't feel comfortable meeting here in a bar on Beale Street. And that woman is being lewd.

**COUNCILMAN:** You two... ah... let's...

**JONES:** Ain't nothin' wrong wit dat woman, 'cept she feel like dancin' out what on her mine. Peepas does dat all da time heah. Somethin' happen, day don't unnastan it, day come dance, cry, fall down; and den day goes home an' go ta bed.

**BILLINGS:** I shouldn't be seen in this kind of place at all.

JONES:  Rev. Billings, dis kinda place where Jesus fount his peepas, accordin' ta da Bible.

BILLINGS:  I'm well aware of what the Bible says. It also says something about dens of iniquity.

COUNCILMAN:  Look, gentlemen, we didn't come together to bicker over theology.

*[A MAN approaches the table and motions for JONES to speak with him privately. JONES steps a short distance with the Man.]*

JONES:  'Scuse me... Whas hapnin', Brotha Kenny?

KENNY:  Fightin' the lizard for leavin's. I knowed you havin' a impo'tant meetin' 'n all. But things tuck a ton fah da worse with da wife. Stroke come back an' I hada put her in the hospital.

JONES:  Oh Lawd, how is she?

KENNY:  She got ta stay deah, and day axin' fah money. Don't git pay 'till Friday, but hospital wants day payday now. Anything you kin let me have, I 'preciate.

JONES:  Heah's twenty. Union ain't got much in the welfare fund, but see Brotha Rock; he chairman of the welfare committee. On Sunday, I ask Rev. Moore do a special collection.

KENNY:  Danky, Brotha Jones. I knew if I spoke to you personal, I'd git some hep. May Gawd bless ya. I won't hole ya up no moe.

JONES:  Night, Brotha Kenny. I'm prayin' fah ya wife.

*[JONES returns to the table where BILLINGS and the COUNCILMAN wait impatiently.]*

BILLINGS:  Look, can we get this over?

JONES:  Git what ova?

COUNCILMAN:  T.O., the Mayor says you and a few men are

going on strike. Is this true?

JONES: The Mayor done plugged into the bush telegraph real good, ain't he?

COUNCILMAN: T.O., if five people get together to do something in Memphis, the whole town knows.

JONES: Why you suddenly concern about a strike?

BLUESMAN: Because I live here too. Those people at City Hall are not going to recognize a union. I know those people!

COUNCILMAN: They smile and invite you over for barbecue, and when you get there, they put the barbecue sauce on you. For them it's 1850. Certain ideas are traditional to them. You know and I know they're not going to give up tradition. You've got to be less confrontational. Forget the strike, sit down and talk to the Mayor.

JONES: I am gon' talk to 'im. I'm gon' tell 'im we gon' strike if conditions don't change. And den he do what he got ta do and I do what I got ta do. Das how life go.

BILLINGS: Are you aware of how much suffering you'll be bringing on those eight hundred men and their families? I thought you cared about your "union" brothers.

JONES: I do care, das why we strikin'. Will you help feed the strikers and take up a weekly collection for dem in yo' church?

BILLINGS: I should say not!

JONES: Why not?

BILLINGS: I've never seen any of your men in my church.

JONES: What dat got ta do wit grits and gravy for hungry chilrens?

COUNCILMAN: If you call off this strike, I'll personally intercede with the Mayor and...

JONES: Naw, da Mayor got ta recognize the union and deal

wit us legal, none of dis personal intercede.

BILLINGS:   I think your stubborness is due to your turbulent personal life.

JONES:   Whatchu mean by dat, Rev.?

BILLINGS:   The "bush telegraph" says you and she fight all the time. And you're so busy with the union and other vices that you ignore your family.

JONES:   Sound to me like you been out shaking the bushes like a common, lowlife coon trying ta shake blackberries.

*[BILLINGS gets up and stomps out without a word.]*

COUNCILMAN:   Jones, in Memphis, you need the churches. That man is with the Ministers' Coalition. He could get some important ministers to negotiate with the Mayor on your behalf. You just insulted him.

JONES:   *[Sarcastically.]* Since he a man of God, maybe he kin fine it in his heart to forgive me. And the Ministers' Co'lishon ain't on strike, we is.

COUNCILMAN:   Jones, what do you want?

JONES:   I already 'splained what da union wan...

COUNCILMAN:   I'm asking, what do you want? You are the union. You founded it; you're the president.

JONES:   Oh, I see. Well, let me put it dis way: My great grandaddy was a slave in Alabama. He was trained to be a blacksmith. Got tired a bein' a slave. He runaway to Memphis. Dat's still South, but he ain't wanna leave da South, and he don't want nobody ta know he a runaway slave. What you reckon he do?

COUNCILMAN:   Jones, I... This is not what I...

JONES:   What you reckon he do?

COUNCILMAN:   I don't know.

JONES:   He pretend he a slave. He work on blacksmith jobs

and git money like he hired out for rent by a master. He pretend he belong to a certain sea captain. Keep his house fa him when he at sea. Great grandaddy make up a whole story 'bout dis sea captain. Say he run a ship dat sail to India and China. Now, dere ain't no sea captain, of course. Never was. But folks don't know it. My great grandaddy knowed how to tell a great story.

COUNCILMAN: Yes, fine, but...

JONES: Let me roun' off my remarks. Oncet a year, a white man'd come visit grandaddy. He met great grandaddy in Alabama. Dis white man was living den in Virginia, but he ain't care nothin' 'bout no slavery. He against it. He like my great grandaddy. Become his fren. Da white man pretend he da sea captain. He walk aroun' Memphis wit great grandaddy and order him about like a master, and let everybody see. Den the white man go back to Virginia. And great grandaddy keep on pretending he a slave so's he could be free.

COUNCILMAN: I see, but...

JONES: Dere's mo'. Well, it turn out dat da white man was really a mulatto who was pretending ta be white in Virginia.

COUNCILMAN: Fine, but what's the point?

JONES: I ain't got to da point yet.

COUNCILMAN: You haven't?

JONES: Now, two generations lata, here come my daddy.

COUNCILMAN: [Resigned.] What happened to your daddy, T.O.?

JONES: My daddy was the youngest chile out of nineteen chilrens. He become a minister who wuck in a lumbermill. Daddy wucked in the lumbermill 'till about 1935. Dat's Depression. Daddy got let go dat year. Day let him go 'cause da fo'eman got some nephew coming from Europe what need a job. So daddy left dat job and he chop cotton until he die. Now dere's me.

COUNCILMAN:  Yes, you at last.

JONES:  At last. I come 'long and wucked for Sanitation Department. Times done change. I ain't got ta pretend I'm a slave so I can be free. And I'm tired a bein' let go anytime somebody feel like it. Back in '63 day fired me 'cause I start a union. But I'm still here, and so is the union. Dat's what I want. I want a union where you ain't got ta pretend nothin', and you cain't be let go just 'cause somebody else want yo' job. I'm gon' make da Mayor recognize my union.

COUNCILMAN:  T.O., I think you better get prepared for a whole lot of trouble.

*[Lights and Images crossfade with the previous storefront church where REV. MOORE speaks as JONES approaches and enters the lighted playing space.]*

BLUESMAN:  *[In blues mode.]*

WHOLE LOTTA TROUBLE HEADING THIS WAY
WHOLE LOTTA TROUBLE HEADING THIS WAY
YEAH, WHOLE LOTTA TROUBLE HEADING THIS WAY

*[The voice of REV. MOORE cuts in and interrupts BLUESMAN who fades to silence. Moore holds a few sheets of paper, a manila envelope and a pen. He wears workclothes, his lunch bucket is nearby. JONES has entered by now. It is Tuesday evening.]*

MOORE:  He telling you right, Brotha Jones. If you go looking for trouble, it's easy to find.

JONES:  Rev. Moore, I hears what you saying, but, say fah'ninstance...

MOORE:  That's another thing right there: You can't be going off tellin' some instance about what happened to yo' uncle's mule in Pulaski, Tennessee. Lawd ha'mercy! Keep it simple!

JONES: But if you coulda heard dem men's explainin' day complaints...

BLUESMAN: I don't hafta hear their complaints. I got a gang of sanitation workers in my congregation. Just lost two, remember?

MOORE: I know what they feeling and I support them a hundred percent, but the way I got it written out here is your best approach. Get in there, talk straight with the man, state your demands and ask him to respond.

JONES: Seem like he already respond, just like a snake in da backalley.

MOORE: Lawd ha'mercy! Don't walk up in the snake's office and call him no snake. You asking 'im to bite you. You got to charm a snake, see? We talking sho'nuff politics now. Leave the snake some hole he can crawl out. Don't block all the holes or you can't get out either.

JONES: Well, I do mah bes', but dat Mayor need a good preachin' to.

MOORE: Maybe he do, but the Mayor is Episcopalian, see? And you can't be preaching to no Episcopalian. Soon as you start sweatin' and shoutin', they fall apart. I've seen that with my own eyes! Lawd ha'mercy!

*[He and JONES snicker at that.]*

JONES: Rev. Moore, you's a complete mess.

MOORE: I'm gon' be a mess if I don't get to work right now. All that cotton coming to the warehouse tonight. Gotta be unloaded, and I already miss two nights this week 'cause I had ta bury those two men and do family counseling. *[Mimicking.]* "Don't let it happen again," my foreman said. Can you imagine? Don't let anybody die because I've got to unload a boat fulla cotton. Told the man I'm a preacher and I go where the Lord calls me to shepherd His flock.

JONES:  Amen. When you gon' quit dat crane operator job; you always complainin' 'bout runnin' dat crane.

MOORE:  When the Lawd say quit, I quit. I figure the Lawd gon' tell me ta quit soon as I get a big enough congregation. That's according to the Doctrine of Secularistic Nonsecularism which comes from the School of Multiple Reality Fusion.

JONES:  Yeah, well, I unnastan' da confusion part alright.

MOORE:  Then you understand more than me. Reality, Brotha Jones. Reality is the only order that exists; all you got to do is figure out what reality is, then act accordingly, with moral integrity as your guide. They didn't teach me that at the Seminary; learned it on the street.

JONES:  What is you tryin' ta say to me?

MOORE:  Dreams cost you more than anything else in the world. I want a big church, you want a union. We both have to stay on top of things, follow reality, and, as Rev. Powell up in New York say: Keep the faith.

JONES:  I unnastan' dat.

MOORE:  [Pause, hand up to ear.]  Right now I hear the Lawd calling me; He say: "Get yo' butt to work." Lawd ha'mercy! So you take this paper and study it real good before you speak with the Mayor tomorrow.

JONES:  I will, and, Rev., me and da mens thank you for yo precious time.

MOORE:  [A bit sadly.]  Praise da Lawd for that much!

[The Lights and Images shift to the streets where JONES, accompanied by the BLUESMAN, walks home. The BLUESMAN plays a kind of walking blues that is both sad and foreboding. The images are a collage of black ghetto darkness, *closed storefronts, boarded up windows, dilapidated, jerry-built buildings.* JONES *carries the envelope. Two objects are thrown from the darkness and land at his feet, a cheap suitcase tied with a rope and a tattered U.S. Navy dufflebag. He stops and begins squinting into the surrounding blackness. The* BLUESMAN *continues playing but very low, occasionally punctuating the ensuing conversation with bluesy guitar sounds, sometimes discordant, atonal flatted fifths.]*

JONES: Alice Mae, you ain't had ta do all dis.

ALICE: *[Voice from the blackness.]* Ollie, I done mo' den dat. I changed all da locks too.

JONES: Woman, couldn't ya wait 'till the mornin'? Where I'm 'sposed ta go dis time a night?

*[Dim lights rise momentarily on* ALICE MAE, *a big boned, sad-looking woman. The lights will periodically rise and dim on her during her lines. It gives the illusion that she appears and disappears and in different locations throughout the scene.* JONES *turns and speaks towards her new location each time she momentarily appears. Photo images of her from happier days with T.O. can be used here if necessary. These images can appear and disappear in various locations around the playing space. His life with her is ephemeral; they are married in name only.]*

BLUESMAN: I know dat's a lie. You know where you goin' alright.

ALICE: You know just what she look like. Go wallow in the mud wit dat pig you was dancin' with the otha night, whoever she is! Or go to hell, if you want! She look like she come from hell anyhow!

JONES: Look here, Alice Mae, you been tryin' ta accuse me of...

ALICE: *[Viciously, on the verge of tears.]* Nigga please! Don't even start to shape yo' mouth into a lie.

*[JONES is stunned with the truth of what she says, drops his head. ALICE disappears.]*

JONES:  Seems you coulda at least talk to me 'foe you do all dis. You gon' put me out my house and not even talk to me!

ALICE:  *[From the blackness.]* We cain't talk no more. All we do is fight and scream. Cain't do that around the chilren no moe. Day done suffer enough, and so have I. Go stay in the union hall.

*[Dim lights momentarily rise on her in a different location.]*

ALICE:  Tell the union to cook yo' dinner and wash yo clothes. See how much the union love you. That union is all you ever care about. We don't count. You ain't da kinda man who care about his wife and chilrens. You ain't dat kinda man atall.

*[Lights out on her.]*

JONES:  Don't you tell no lie neither! Dem chilrens ain't never been hungry and day got clothes on day back and a shack over day heads. Don't tell me I don't care about mah chilrens. I ain't gon' hear dat!

ALICE:  *[From the blackness.]* You ain't gon' hear nothin' nobody say now. You think you a big leader or somethin'. Thomas Oliver Jones, President of Local 1733.

*[Dim lights rise on her.]*

ALICE:  Hmph! I was witchu when you was hustling pool in the poolhalls, when you was out on the streets scheming. When day used to call you Ollie da Octapus 'cause you had yo' hands in every hustle on the streets. See, don't talk no stuff to me. I know what happened. I done read you for years. I know plenty 'bout you, especially yo' promises. You done made promises to plenty women. They talkin', see? And them promises you made to me? I'm still waitin' on a decent house wit a yard. I been waiting 15 years. Look like me and yo' chilrens go from bad to worse and worser and all you think about is a buncha mens totin' garbage. Give dem half yo' paycheck, nevamine yo' family! Das fine and noble, Ollie, but look at the garbage I been totin' all dese years! Yo' garbage!

*[Lights fade on her.]*

BLUESMAN: *[Hurled into the blackness.]* Alright, you want me tell ya I ain't no saint? I ain't neva met nobody wit two legs dat was. All you saints hiding in the darkness behind yo' doors, all you saints listening to me right now. Come out and show me what a saint look like!

JONES: I done eat dirt too, but I still ain't dirt. I'm just a man. Dem buncha mens totin' garbage stayed by me when day fired me in '63. Rememba? We ain't had two pennies ta rub tagetha. Rememba? Rememba when da mens took up collection every week, branged us groceries, branged us clothes, paid da light bill, an' whatinsoeva we needed? While I'm wuckin' any kinda job I could git, includin' hustlin' when I had ta, dem garbage totin' mens toted you all ova town ta do ya shoppin'. Day come by when da chilrens git sick. Day show me day respeck us, loved us. Day remember how hard I fight fah dem. Sho, I love da union.

*[Dim lights rise on her.]*

ALICE: Then carry yo' ass to the union and git you some lovin', 'cause you sho ain't gittin' none here.

JONES: Don't talk to me like dat, bitch! Dat's my house and I'm comin' in it. I got wuck ta...

ALICE: Nigga, I swear befo'e my God, you try to come in this house tonight, me and you gon' fight like the hounds of hell! Ambalance gon' carry one of us outta here tonight! I swear befo'e my God!

*[Lights fade out on her.]*

JONES:  Alice Mae, listen ta reason: Dis union bidness somethin' I hafta do. I ain't no rich man kin buy mah way into history books, an' I ain't no scholar kin talk his way into dem. Da union is what I got, it's what all black mens got. Maybe it's all da chance we got ta earn respeck. Woman, I got eight hunded mens dependin' on me; I cain't quit da union!

*[Dim lights rise on her.]*

ALICE:  *[In weary tears.]* I don't want you ta do nothin', but carry yo bags to somebody else doe. Das all I want. Some peace. Das all I want, Ollie, some womanpeace right now. I'm sorry, Ollie, but it's what I have ta do.

JONES:  *[After a pause, pulling out some bills.]* Well, I guess day ain't nothin' moe ta say. I ain't got but a few dollas, but you kin...

ALICE:  I don't want yo last dolla, Ollie, but try to rememba me and da chilrens when you git paid, okay? Das all I axe, okay?

JONES:  Okay. Alice Mae?

ALICE:  *[Hopeful of reconciliation.]* Yes, Ollie?

JONES:  I'll be stayin' down at the Lorraine Motel in case you need me.

ALICE:  *[Bitterly disappointed.]* Okay, Ollie. The Lorraine Motel.

*[He picks up his bags and starts to trudge away, the BLUESMAN leading. He looks back, shakes his head and walks into the blackness. The BLUESMAN plays a walking blues informed by an immediate sadness and subdued rage. Lights and Images shift to the MAYOR'S "office" space, a desk and two chairs. Music fades out. It is early Thursday evening. He sits busily scribbling. JONES, in a suitjacket and tie and carrying a nearly empty*

*duffle bag, enters. The* MAYOR *gets up to greet him, hand heartily extended which* JONES *grasps. The* BLUESMAN *smiles knowingly and takes a seat in the shadows.]*

MAYOR:  It's been awhile, Mr. Jones.

JONES:  Yeah, reckon so.

MAYOR:  Have a seat.

JONES:  Thank you, Mr. Mayor.

MAYOR:  I don't believe I've seen you since the Sanitation Dept. family picnic back in what? '65 was it?

JONES:  Believe it was, Mr. Mayor.

MAYOR:  *[Recalling.]* Yes, it was. You were there with your family I recall. What's that oldest one's name, Bubba or something like that?

JONES:  Naw, Bubba da second one. He long about twelve years old now. He smellin' his manhood coming on.

MAYOR:  Twelve? Isn't it remarkable how fast children grow?

JONES:  Yeah, I 'speck das da truf.

MAYOR:  Hard to keep up with them. Expensive raising children nowadays, isn't it?

JONES:  I 'speck so. I never did meet yo' family, but I pray da Lawd day doin' fine.

MAYOR:  *[Perfunctorily.]* Oh, the missus is just fine. Thank you. Jones, as you may recall, I'm a frank man. How'd you like to be foreman over the truck drivers in all the colored wards?

JONES:  *[Confused at first.]* Foreman?

MAYOR:  Yes, foreman. You'd be making almost $4.00 an hour. With that kind of money a man could make enough to take care of his family pretty well.

JONES:  *[Understanding the bribe offer, tense.]* I ain't come lookin' fa no job, I got one, and dat job brang me here.

MAYOR:  And what job is that?

JONES:  *[Pulling out the papers.]*  I come to pree-sent this list of union demands.

MAYOR:  "Union demands," indeed! The very words are offensive to some people hereabouts.

JONES:  Well, Mr. Mayor, I spec' we ain't lookin' ta be offensive atall. But we feel it is our right ta has better wages and better workin' condition. What I got listed here say: We the Public Works Employees of Memphis, Tennessee, do hereby demand recognition for the American Federation of State, County and Municipal Employees as da legal collective bargainin' agent for the Public Works Department of the City of...

MAYOR:  You memorized it?

JONES:  I study it, sho. I got a copy fah you also.

MAYOR:  Well, you don't have to recite it me. I know how to read, Mr. Jones.

JONES:  I was just makin' sho' you ain't miss none of it. It's betta when ya say a thing. Den peepas knows what you meaning, 'cause day see yo face and know dat you mean bidness.

MAYOR:  You've convinced me that you mean *[Correcting.]* "business." So, what's on your mind, Mr. Jones?

JONES:  We fidden ta go strike come Monday 'lessen our demands are met.

MAYOR:  Is this what you've decided?

JONES:  It's what da union decided.

MAYOR:  What union? The city recognizes no labor union and has never officially done so since 1819 when Memphis was founded.

JONES:  1819 gone, and we fidden ta strike.

MAYOR:  "Fidden'" or no, as the primary representative of the citizens of this community, I am informing you that a strike of city employees is illegal and anyone who violates the law will be prosecuted and jailed. Do I make myself clear?

JONES: Let me be clear too.

*[JONES begins undressing which first perplexes the* MAYOR *and then amuses him.* JONES *strips off his outer garments and dons workman clothes.* BLUESMAN *playfully strums "stripper" music during the undressing. When he's done, he turns to the* MAYOR.*]*

JONES: I'm ready ta go ta jail now.

MAYOR: I beg your pardon?

JONES: I'm ready ta go ta jail now. Monday we gon' be on strike. And da injunction still running.

MAYOR: Mr. Jones, your striptease was certainly dramatic, though not titillating. But I can assure you that no one need go to jail.

JONES: When the injunction break, somebody got ta go ta jail, and I 'speck it's me, since I'm president.

MAYOR: But why do you want to go to jail?

JONES: I don't wanna go ta jail, but da law is da law.

BLUESMAN: Mr. Jones, when I was Public Works Commissioner in '62, I gave you people due consideration. You and I and a few others sat down and talked.

MAYOR: There was no public fuss, no need to strike. You remember? In fact, I personally promoted several colored men to truck driver. Now, I can assure you that I'm the same fair man now as I was then. We can reach an equitable agreement without...

JONES: *[Interrupting.]* Mayor, one man good, anotha man bad. Cain't be waitin' and hopin' we git a good man. We wants it wrote out in 'greement wit the union, so's we kin have good even when it's bad runnin' Public Works Department.

MAYOR: *[Impatient, exasperated.]* Let me line up the facts for you. One...

JONES: *[Interrupting.]* Ain't matta how you line up da facts if dat line don't lead to da union.

MAYOR: *[Burst of anger.]* I will not be subject to anyone's demands. I have the interests of this city to protect and, believe me, Mr. Jones, I will protect them.

JONES: *[Angry, but cool.]* Mr. Mayor, you lookin' at a impo'-tent part of yo' city right now. Me and da mens I repre-sents. You 'sposed ta protect all da peepas. I 'speck sanitation workers need plenty protection, totin' all dat garbage.

MAYOR: Maybe you better consider the options open to me. There are hundreds of men out there who would appre-ciate an opportunity to be employed by the Public Works Department.

JONES: *[Openly angry, standing.]* Scabs? You put on scabs?

MAYOR: *[Standing and close to shouting.]* New sanitation work-ers is what I'd call them. We can't allow garbage to accu-mulate. That's endangering public health. I won't stand for that! You understand me, Jones?

JONES: Well, da mens cain't stan' no moe fah dese conditions. We shall not be moved! You unnastan' me, Mr. Mayor?

MAYOR: I can speak English.

JONES: I ain't talkin' 'bout whatchu speakin', I'm talkin' 'bout whatchu hearin'! You ain't hearin' me. Da mens meetin' in the Retail Clerk's union hall rat now waitin' fah word from me. If I goes back dere and tell 'em ta withhold ser-vice, day gon' sho'nuff do dat. So, you better sit yo'sef down and listen ta me. I'm in control here!

MAYOR: *[Derisive chortle.]* In control, is it? I'll tell you what.

I'll go over to that meeting and personally explain what I've been trying...

JONES:  You will do no such a thing. Dem mens won't hear a word you say 'lessen I authorizes you ta speak.

MAYOR:  Unless you what me?

JONES:  I believe you heard me.

MAYOR:  *[Out of control.]* I don't need some nigger to authorize me to do anything.

*[JONES slaps the MAYOR's face resoundingly which literally knocks the MAYOR on his ass. The MAYOR is both emotionally and physically stunned and then a bit fearful as JONES hovers over him.]*

JONES:  I ain't no nigga! I am a man. You hear what I say? I AM A MAN!

*[The MAYOR scrambles backward to his feet as he tries to recover and regain his composure. JONES glares at him. The BLUES-MAN has gotten up and struck an ominous chord.]*

MAYOR:  You get out of my office now!

*[They stare at each other for a moment. Then JONES storms out, the BLUESMAN trailing. The MAYOR picks up the phone. On a chord from the BLUESMAN Lights and Images shift to JONES' room at the Lorraine Motel, a space with a chair and a nightstand. WEATHERFORD and MOORE, in black suits and collars, nervously pace as they await JONES. The images are of the exterior of the old Lorraine Motel and the surrounding neighborhood in 1968, dilapidated, weathered, worn, old and bitter. It's Friday evening. JONES enters and the ministers pounce on him. WEATHERFORD speaks in a precise British accent although he is Canadian.]*

MOORE:  You cain't be going 'round slapping the mayor upside his head! Lawd ha'mercy!

BLUESMAN:  You've unwisely increased his intransigence.

**WEATHERFORD:** Yes, I fear that you've unwisely increased his intransigence.

**MOORE:** I told you not to get emotional around no Espiscopalian! Lawd ha'mercy! Teach me how to pray!

**JONES:** Beggin' yo' pardon, reverends, but whas done is done. Right now I got to figure out the next move.

**WEATHERFORD:** We've got to marshall effective community support, starting with the Memphis Ministers Coalition.

**MOORE:** Rev. Weatherford, with the exception of you and maybe a few others, I don't get along so well with that coalition. They have social status on the brain.

**WEATHERFORD:** I understand and sympathize, Brother Moore, but they're greatly influential. I knew of a similar situation in Toronto. That time it was a local tribe of Native Americans whose treaty had been unilaterally abrogated by a group of real estate developers. The ministers first resisted, but the spirit of Jesus eventually won their hearts, and, subsequently, the battle.

**JONES:** But dat co'lition acts like da union man is dirt.

**MOORE:** Rev. Weatherford, you haven't been in Memphis too long. Let me explain something: Lots of those ministers in the Coalition  have those big church buildings, the ones that white folks left behind when they ran from urban renewal. Catholics, Presbyterians, Baptists, you name it, all those white Christians. They picked up their Christian belongings and sensibilities and left because they didn't want to live next to "Nigras."  And it look like when the black ministers from the Coalition got in those abandoned white churches, they started breathing the same stale air.

**JONES:** Amen. Back in '63 and later in '66; we was tryin' ta strike. The co'lition told us to stop. In fact, one minister rolled his Cadillac down to the Retail Clerks Hall where we was meetin'. Da man got down on his knees and asked da Lawd to evick us.

**MOORE:** Lawd ha'mercy!

**JONES:** Dat co'lition, it got problems.

**WEATHERFORD:** Indeed it has, but the Lord works in mysterious ways, His wonders to perform. We need a show of faith, I'd say, as in Isaiah, Chapter 1, Verse 18: "Come now let us reason together... though your sins be as scarlet, they shall be white as snow..."

**MOORE:** Brother Weatherford, something about that verse from Isaiah always bothered me.

**WEATHERFORD:** Oh really?

**MOORE:** Really, but that's another story. Truthfully, he right, T.O., we have to find support wherever we can. But, Brotha Weatherford, you take on the Coalition. I'll handle the Black Ministerial Alliance; I attended theological seminary with a few of them.

**JONES:** Fine. Ya'll got da ministers, but rememba: Dis is a labor movement, not no prayer meetin'. I'm runnin' things.

**MOORE:** Man, let us worry about the ministers. But what about the rest of the community?

**JONES:** I know almost everybody who is somebody on Beale Street. We need day support too. And the NAACP too. I'm gonna bring dis city to its knees.

**WEATHERFORD:** What about the other labor organizations in Memphis?

**JONES:** I personally know Bill Ross. He sit on the Memphis Labor Council; that's AFL-CIO peepas. Yesah, I got dat covered.

**WEATHERFORD:** Splendid! We'll need their help if the Mayor proves unequivocally intractable.

**MOORE:**  Do you talk like that when you preach in your church?

**WEATHERFORD:**  Well... I... not exactly.

**MOORE:**  I hope not.

**WEATHERFORD:**  What do you mean?

**MOORE:**  Just offering brotherly advice: Language you use can't bring the spirit in a church like yours.

**WEATHERFORD:**  I suppose you're referring to the fact that my congregation is all Negro.

**MOORE:**  Exactly. And I hear your congregation is shrinking.

**WEATHERFORD:**  A few of the flock have strayed, but we're laboring to...

**MOORE:**  Listen to me. You fairly new in this town. A British man raised up in Canada. You're an anomaly like they mighta said at Crozier Theological Seminary. And, don't take it wrong, it's all right to be an anomaly, but if you want to be a preacher with a Negro congregation, you got to speak a different language. The spirit ain't gon' get into the people through *[Mimicking.]* "unequivocally intractable." You need to study services at a Pentecostal or Baptist or Church of God in Christ, like me. Of course, I speak as a brother in Christ.

**WEATHERFORD:**  *[Poking fun at himself.]* I certainly do appreciate your brotherly concern; I've been struggling to rid my sermons of tedious intellectual discourse, and I am resolutely striving towards an effective homiletic permutation, as it were.

**MOORE:**  *[Laughing with him.]* Yeah, we can see that.

*[As the BLUESMAN strums an ironic chord, Lights and Images shift to NAACP offices where MISS SECRETARY waits. A huge image of W.E.B. DuBois dominates. Other images are of various civil rights protest activities of the '60's. JONES*

*merely walks into her space from his previous position. The dialogue may begin before he enters. It is now Saturday afternoon.]*

SECRETARY:  The NAACP is a civil rights organization, not a labor advocate group.

JONES:  Day violatin' our right to strike 'cause we public works.

SECRETARY:  T.O., it's more complicated than that. You said that they treat the workers badly because they are Negro.

JONES:  I said that, sho'. Das a problem. But we ain't striking to be Negro, we striking for a union. Put da union in place first and den work out da mechanics 'bout bein' Negro.

SECRETARY:  A good labor lawyer is what you need for that. You should contact your international for that kinda help.

JONES:  International ain't got two cents in dis quarta yet.

SECRETARY:  You mean they don't know you're goin' on strike?

JONES:  We cain't be waitin' fah peepas sittin' behine desks up North to tell us when we kin strike. We at the battle front, not dem.

SECRETARY:  T.O., I think you have to get the international's approval. I mean, your local is affiliated. You're a paid organizer. You need their support.

JONES:  Well, I 'tend ta call dem soon as we get da strike goin'.

SECRETARY:  That's not what I mean.

JONES:  Das what we mean.

SECRETARY:  *[Sighing heavily in resignation.]* Are you planning to picket or anything?

JONES:  We havin' a 'mergency meetin' with the Mayor's Advisory Bode tomorrow. If day don't go 'long wit my demands, then we strike.

SECRETARY:  *[Laughs somewhat derisively.]* Tomorrow! Why,

that's utterly ridiculous, there's no time to... a few days more would...

BLUESMAN AND JONES: *[Angrily, sensing condescension.]* It's all the time we got! Do da bes' you can.

SECRETARY: But, T.O., okay. All right... I understand all that, honest I really do. My origins are humble too, but I can't get my board together on such short notice.

JONES: *[Rising to leave.]* We ain't waitin' on nobody.

SECRETARY: I'm with you, but you have to trust me. This is a complex situation. It'll take some complex maneuvering, you know?

*[Lights and Images shift to a City Hall meeting room again. It is Saturday evening. The MAYOR and CHIEF OF POLICE watch and listen to the COLLABORATOR.]*

MAYOR: Is there anything else we should know about?

COLLABORATOR: Well, not much else, Mr. Mayor. 'Cept maybe you might be interested to know that Jones been staying over at the Lorraine Motel ever since his wife threw him out. That's where Martin Luther King stays whenever he comes to Memphis. Could be a coincidence or not. But since Hoover thinks that King is definitely hooked up with the Communists, it's something we feel we should keep an eye on.

MAYOR: Fine, see that you do. Chief?

CHIEF: You're dismissed for now.

MAYOR: I won't be at the meeting with the so-called strikers. I intend to monitor events from my office. The Senior Negro Councilman will preside. I trust you've taken precautions?

CHIEF: Of course. *[Handing him a pistol.]* And keep this with you. Just a further precaution.

*[Lights and Images cut to the special meeting. A screen says: FEB. 22, CITY COUNCIL CHAMBERS. JONES, MOORE and the CHIEF wait expectantly. The BLUESMAN plays gospel style riffs on "We Shall Not Be Moved," a traditional spiritual. Flashbulbs go off. We hear sounds of hundreds of grumbling men in a cavernous meeting chamber. A large city seal of Memphis dominates the room. The SENIOR NEGRO COUNCILMAN enters, sits under the seal, and raps his gavel to begin the meeting. A few flashbulbs go off. The music fades to silence.]*

COUNCILMAN:  Let it be understood that the Advisory Board's purpose here is to get information and make recommendations to the full City Council. No decisions can be made this morning.

JONES:  Den whatchu call us here for? We need a decision now!

*[We hear sounds of applause and cheers of support. The COUNCILMAN is shaken.]*

COUNCILMAN:  We've heard Mr. Jones. Would anyone else like to contribute?

*[JONES looks sternly at the men which apparently intimidates them. He turns back to the COUNCILMAN.]*

JONES:  We say we wants ta be recognized as a union now!

COUNCILMAN:  I just saw a few hands go up. Let the men speak for themselves. We want to hear directly from their mouths!

JONES:  We speakin' wit one voice tonight.

COUNCILMAN:  *[To the MEN.]*  Look, you men have the authority of the Board to back you up. Don't be intimidated by this man's rudeness and disrespect for your intelligence.

JONES:  Onliest one rude here is you! You has no respeck!

MOORE:  He's the elected representative of the union. He speaks for the men.

**COUNCILMAN:** Unacceptable! The city does not recognize that union and therefore will not entertain the showboat ranting of some so-called representative.

**BLUESMAN:** Rantin'! You wanna hear some rantin'? Let me tell 'bout that city seal you got hanging over yo' head.

**JONES:** See dat steamboat? It bring slaves up and downriver for trading. The cotton boll? Dat's what da slaves pick ta make a few peepas rich. That oak leaf is where day tied the slave to beat him or where they hanged him. Used ta whip ya wit dem oak sticks too. Dat piece a machinery? Dat's the wheel of progress dat grine the slave up. Da Civa War ova, but we still fighting against slavery. Chop cotton for three dollas a day or tote garbage for one dolla and sixty cent a hour. Da union come here ta finally stop slavery.

**COUNCILMAN:** Out of order! Be silent or be held in contempt.

**JONES:** Since when we in coat and who made you judge?

**COUNCILMAN:** I'm warning you... I...

**JONES:** We don't take orders from a flunkey. Where da Mayor hidin'?

**COUNCILMAN:** This hearing is adjourned! Clear the chambers!

**JONES:** Yeah, we'll clear the chambers alright. Let's have us a parade! Let's clear outta here and have us a parade. We'll picket the whole town. Let's take our grievance to the world!

[JONES *and the* MEN *break into a spontaneous and spirited reprise of "We Shall Not Be Moved," lyrics appropriately adapted to the immediate circumstances. Led by* JONES *the* MEN *begin filing out. The* CHIEF *and the* COUNCILMAN *angrily exit. Lights and Images crossfade. Sounds of street traffic and a public demonstration drift in. It is the afternoon of Feb. 22.* JONES *leads the men from the "Council Chamber" to the "street". The images are of a street down which* JONES, MOORE *and* WEATHERFORD *enter in single file as if in a parade/demonstration. Images should be photographs of the actual demonstrations and marches that were ongoing during the strike. There especially should be photos of the men carrying signs that all say I AM A MAN. These photos and film clips of same can be obtained from the Mississippi Valley Collection at the Memphis State Library and/or from Eugene Withers, the then photographer of the Tri-State Defender.* SEVERAL INVADERS *march through on the periphery in a doubletime lockstep. The music fades out. Near* JONES, MOORE *and* WEATHERFORD *walk* TWO POLICEMEN, *one black and one white. They wear riot gear and carry gas masks, shields and batons. They have a walkie-talkie from which we hear occasional static. The images will change appropriately with the ensuing activity. The* BLUESMAN *strolls by playing improvisationally, receives tips in his cup.]*

**WEATHERFORD:**  Seems to be some delay up front.

**JONES:**  Probably traffic. Day should halt traffic for us 'stead of da otha way 'round.

**MOORE:**  Since this march is spontaneous, we have to accept delays because the police are playing it by ear too. We shoulda planned this. Something ain't right. You think there's trouble up there?

**WEATHERFORD:**  *[Mischievously.]* There's about twelve ministers at the head of the march. Their presence assures a modicum of sobriety.

**MOORE:**  Indubitably! Perhaps!

**JONES:**  Lawson's up there with them.

**WEATHERFORD:**  Ah, Rev. Lawson, the great philospher champion of nonviolence. I understand he's a personal friend of Martin Luther King.

JONES: Yeah, he King's main strategy man. Ain't got nothin' ta worry about.

MOORE: *[Muttering aloud.]* Maybe. I dunno.

JONES: Rev. Moe, ain't been no trouble yet and we ain't lookin' for none.

MOORE: But I seen some of them Invaders lurking around. I hear they talk a lot of revolutionary stuff.

JONES: Let dem Invaders talk. Day only talkin' and we only walkin'.

WEATHERFORD: What in Heaven's name are Invaders?

MOORE: It's a gang of young hotheads that claims to be revolutionaries. Hmph! They got their name from a TV program called Invaders.

WEATHERFORD: A TV program?

MOORE: As the Lord is my witness. Those people make me nervous hanging around here.

JONES: Don't worry 'bout no Invaders; day ain't got two cents in this quarta. Everything is unda con... Wait a minute. Looka dere.

*[JONES stares intently at one of the POLICEMEN, calls out to him and approaches him.]*

JONES: Peewee Slocum? Is that Peewee, Jasper Slocum's baby brotha?

*[The BLACK POLICEMAN pulls off his sunglasses, recognizes and smiles.]*

BLACK POLICEMAN (BP): Thomas Oliver Jones, I'll be damned. Ain't this somethin'!

*[They laughingly embrace.]*

JONES: Last time I seed you yo' brotha was chasin' you along the river, fidden ta kill you. Said you threw his bike into the Mississippi River.

**BP:** I did and he caught me and beat my butt all the way home.

**JONES:** I ain't never seen no cullud child run dat fast. How is Jasper?

**BP:** Aww, he moved over ta a little town in eastern Tennessee, say he don't like western Tennessee. Uh, Brotha Jones, if you don't mine me axin', how long ya'll gon' be marchin'? My wife folks comin' over today and she got a barbecue all planned.

**JONES:** I don't reckon this one today gon' las' too long. It just grew, sudden. Look here, dis is Rev. Weatherford and Rev. Moore. Day supporting us.

**BP:** Pleased ta make yo' acquaintance, reverends. I been knowin' T.O. since I was almos' a baby. Him and my big brotha was in the Navy together. *[Referring to the other policeman.]* And this is my partner, Jeffrey Cavender.

**WEATHERFORD:** It's certainly a pleasure to make both your acquaintances.

**WHITE POLICEMAN (WP):** *[Removing glasses, shaking hands.]* Likewise, reverends.

**MOORE:** This weather is perfect, Lawd ha'mercy!

**WP:** Supposed to stay this way all day and most of tomorrow.

**WEATHERFORD:** *[Lustily.]* Lord have mercy for that as well.

**MOORE:** Too bad ya'll have to carry all that heavy equipment on a day nice as this.

**BP:** It's our job, ain't got no choice.

**MOORE:** Yeah, duty first, right?

**WP:** Yep, that's about it. Gotta put bread on the table like everybody else.

*[CROWD SOUNDS AHEAD increase and shortly afterwards so does the walkie-talkie static. Suddenly, a CLEAR VOICE blares out from the walkie-talkie.]*

VOICE:  CLEAR THE STREETS! CODE 5! REPEAT: CLEAR THE STREETS! CODE 5!

POLICEMEN:  MOVE! MOVE! MOVE! MOVE! MOVE! MOVE! MOVE! MOVE! MOVE! MOVE!

*[The Lights abruptly reflect an almost surrealistic terrorism. POLICEMEN suddenly don glasses and begin spraying mace into the eyes of everyone. CROWD SOUNDS: PEOPLE yelling, screaming, running. Several people run across the playing space yelling and rubbing their eyes. POLICEMEN spray and club them as they pass. Sirens wail in the distance. Tear gas is released. The COPS put on gas masks. Projected Images change rapidly and reflect what really happened in the actual march of Feb. 22, 1968. The BLUESMAN plays discordantly, wildly as the activity swirls about him. JONES, yelling to the POLICEMEN to stop, tries to fight the POLICEMEN, but is pulled offstage by MOORE who suffers from macing. WEATHERFORD, blinded by the mace, stumbles about in a cloud of teargas. He unbuttons his coat and reaches inside for a hankie. The WHITE COP sees this and yells.]*

WP:  He's got a gun! Watch out!

*[The WHITE COP fires twice, hitting WEATHERFORD in his chest which instantly kills him.]*

POLICEMEN:  MOVE! MOVE! MOVE! MOVE! MOVE! MOVE! MOVE! MOVE!

*[Lights and Images crosscut to interior and exterior shots of the Lorraine Motel, JONES' room. The Music has faded to silence. The BLUESMAN sits in a corner, softly playing a slow, meditative tune. The Sign says: LATE THAT EVENING, LORRAINE HOTEL, JONES' ROOM. JONES is alone, nursing his bruises.]*

MLK'S VOICE:  "...nations are caught up with the drum major instinct. I must be first... God didn't call America to engage in a senseless, unjust war, *[such]* as the war in Vietnam. We are criminals in that war... And we won't stop it because of our pride, and our arrogance as a nation..."

*[The phone rings. The music fades to silence as the lights fade to black on the BLUESMAN.]*

**JONES:** Hello.

**TELEPHONE VOICE:** Is this *the* T.O. Jones?

**JONES:** It is. Who dis?

**VOICE:** T.O. Don't that mean TAKE OUT?

**JONES:** Who is dis?

**VOICE:** I'm a messenger.

**JONES:** From who?

**VOICE:** From people who uphold morality.

**JONES:** Why you call?

**VOICE:** Don't you have two sons?

**JONES:** What you want?

**VOICE:** I saw your sons coming home from school. They always come the same way.

**JONES:** What about my sons?

**VOICE:** They come from a nigger like you; means they're polluted too. Yore whole line got ta be stopped.

**JONES:** You want me—come git me, if you a real man. You know where I'm at, otherwise you ain't shit!

**VOICE:** Well, nigger, in case you don't know it yet, yore dead. And we gon' hack off yore sons balls, just ta make certain yore kind don't propagate. And, speaking of shit, we're gon' cut off yore head and shit in yore mouth. Bye, nigger!

*[He angrily hangs up and nervously dials ALICE MAE. The phone awakens her. Dim lights rise on her in a nightgown.]*

**ALICE:** Hello.

**JONES:** It's Ollie, baby.

**ALICE:** Ollie? Whas wrong? Somethin' wrong, ain't it?

**JONES:** Are the chilrens all right?

**ALICE:** They sleep, like I was. Whas done happen, Ollie?

**JONES:** Make sho' all da does locked, and don't let nobody in.

**ALICE:** The does? What... Ollie, whas wrong? You in trouble 'cause of that parade mess this morning? Ain't you? You hurt or anything?

**JONES:** Yeah, but I'm all right. Just a few bruises. My eyes still itchin' from the mace, but nothin' too bad.

**ALICE:** I saw all dat mess on TV and read 'bout it in da *Scimitar.* Day say ya'll attacked da police and started a riot. Turned over a squad car. Everything.

**JONES:** Well, das freedom of da press fah ya, I reckon. But it had nothin' ta do with da truth. Police car run over some woman's foot. She went ta screaming and everything went outta control. They outright murdered Rev. Weatherford and beat the rest of us. Look, Alice Mae, we can't let the chilrens go to school tomorrow. I'll be over dere in a few minutes and explain.

**ALICE:** They afta you, ain't they? You done gone and riled up white folks, ain't you? They wanna hurt my chilren too, don't they?

**JONES:** Naw, I ain't heard nothin' 'bout dat, but I figures it better ta play it safe 'til we see what they thinkin'. You cain't be too careful when it comes to wild crackers.

**ALICE:** *[Trembling, near tears.]* T.O., don't let them people hurt my chilrens. Don't care what you have to do. Don't let them peepas hurt my chilrens! They been hurt enough. Please Lawd!

**JONES:** Just lock the does good and wait on me. Ya'll safe right now. All right, Alice Mae?

ALICE:  All right, Ollie.

*[Lights out on* ALICE. *Someone pounds on* JONES' *door. He jumps in fright, grabs a piece of furniture as a weapon. The pounding is insistent.]*

VOICE:  Jones, it's brothers in the struggle. Open the door. Jones!

JONES:  Who is it?

VOICE:  It's Swahili, man! Swahili!

*[*JONES *lowers the chair;* SWAHILI *and* CINNAMON, *cum "revolutionary attire," dark glasses, enter, check the place out.* CINNAMON *remains at attention by the door and always walks and stands at attention throughout scenes in which he appears. They each briefly remove glasses when introducing themselves by name; otherwise they'll wear them throughout the play.]*

SWAHILI:  Habari Gani, mzee. Sheikamu! We the Invaders formally greet you in solidarity and brotherly love.

BLUESMAN:  You never met me, but I'm certain you heard of us in the local fascist press.

JONES:  Yeah, I heard of ya. Ya'll got some kinda Black Panther gang goin'.

BLUESMAN:  The wretched of the earth have been bathed in the perception of those who torture them.

SWAHILI:  We captured Africans in America don't know nothin' about ourselves 'cept what we read in the two most racist newspapers in the South. We ain't got nothin' ta do with da Panthers. That's anotha story, but we wit dem in Black Solidarity. *[Unique salute.]* Power to the People!

CINNAMON:  *[Returning salute.]* Powa ta da Peepas!

SWAHILI:  They call me Swahili. This is my podna, Brotha Cinnamon. He's the other half of the body guard contingent assigned to protect you by Commander Whisper. I know you heard about P.J. Whisper!

JONES: Yeah, I believe somebody tole me day read about him too.

SWAHILI: They lied! P.J. Whisper trying to bring knowledge and discipline to the community. He feels the community have the right to defend theyself against enemies by any means necessary. He don't mean no harm to nobody 'bout nothin', just so long as they don't mean no harm to captured Africans in America. That's his whole philosophy in a nutshell. And he got a social program go 'long wit dat.

JONES: What bring ya'll here tonight?

SWAHILI: You represent the only black power move in this city. Everybody else talkin' and walkin' in step to whitey's brass band. You stepped forward and declared yo'self a black man. You a runaway. That's dangerous in Babylon. These crackers fidden ta swoop down on you like a flock of ducks on a fat junebug. You need protection and the Invaders program say protect you at all costs, by any means necessary, even against yo' will if need be. You a asset to the poor, working people. We here to serve and protect you and yo' family from the people who say they're civilized but ack like beasts, even toward one another. We got a squad stationed outside yo' wife home now. And me and Brotha Cinnamon, we stationed outside yo' doe. That's it, mzee. *[Saluting.]* Power to the people.

CINNAMON: *[Saluting JONES.]* Powa ta da peepas!

JONES: You say you got somebody outside my wife doe right now?

SWAHILI: Back and front doe. Where you and yo' family go, we go too. Invaders are thorough. You needs yo' res' after the battle you fought today. But, just ta let you know we serious brothas in the revolution:

*[They open their jackets to reveal pistols and sawed-off double-barrel shotguns.* JONES *is impressed.]*

JONES:  I got me a army at las'!

SWAHILI:  Power to the People!

CINNAMON:  Powa ta da peepas!

*[As lights fade quickly to black on them, a single light rises on the* BLUESMAN. MLK'S VOICE *speaks. The* BLUESMAN *plays softly a refrain of "We Shall Not Be Moved" under his voice.]*

MLK'S VOICE:  "...recognize that he who is greatest among you shall be your servant... it means that everybody can be great. Because everybody can serve... You don't have to have a college degree to serve. You don't have to make your subject and verb agree to serve... You only need a heart full of grace. A soul generated by love. And you can be that servant."

*[As the* BLUESMAN *exits, he continues playing the refrain. Lights to black.]*

*End Act One*

## ACT TWO

*[When houselights are at half, MLK'S VOICE speaks.]*

MLK'S VOICE: "...I'm delighted to see each of you here tonight in spite of a storm warning. You reveal that you are determined to go on anyhow. Something is happening in Memphis, something is happening in our world..."

*[Lights and Images and Sound suggest an airport lounge. It is the next day. The BLUESMAN, wearing a t-shirt that says "BEALE STREET BLUES", stands in a separate light playing softly, his cup available for donations. JOSH SOLOMON, white, CRAIG WILLINS, black, both carrying bags, enter conversing heatedly with JONES. SOLOMON walks with a noticeable limp due a foot deformation from childhood polio. WILLINS carries a copy of the* Commercial Appeal *newspaper. A PERSON enters and dumps garbage nearby and exits. For the remainder of the play, SOMEONE will enter and dump garbage in the playing areas, causing an accumulation that doesn't interfere with the playing too much. Sometimes specific dumping is indicated in the stage directions. The GARBAGE DUMPER will not be noticed by the others. Wherever possible the garbage itself should be used as props, as tables, as chairs, as food, as artifacts, as filing cabinets, etc. Items will actually be taken from garbage cans and piles of garbage by the actors.]*

SOLOMON: Why didn't ya notify us sooner, T.O.?

JONES: Things movin' so fast, wudden no time.

BLUESMAN: Man, would you stop that! Please? What happened to your union discipline?

WILLINS: Team? Remember? You're on a team. You can't just call a strike any ole time you please.

JONES: Why not? We a union, ain't we?

BLUESMAN: You're a union local affiliated with AFSCME. I'm the international representative and he's a top field assistant.

SOLOMON: *[Railing.]* We're your brothers in this struggle. How in hell do we, your brothers, end up being the last to hear about the strike? Some damn newspaper calls me up in New York and wants my comments. "Duhhh", what do I know from a strike in Memphis? I tell 'im, I'm in New York, in my office, spreading cream cheese. They print it!

JONES: *[Angry at Willins.]* And we was down here eatin' garbage! We went on strike! If you cain't support us, den...
*[ANOTHER PERSON enters, dumps garbage nearby and exits.]*

SOLOMON: Relax! We're in your corner. Forgive us. Jetlag, ya know? He dropped everything and came here on twelve hours notice. My wife is having a difficult pregnancy. Touch and go. Not your problem, of course. We're irritated agitators from New York is all. Look, let's drop it. Where are we headed first?

JONES: To yo' hotel, I reckon.

SOLOMON: Can we move out or what? I need to call my wife; we've got an appointment with the Mayor...

JONES: My escort be here d'rectly. Day a few minutes behine schedule.

WILLINS: How about a taxi? They have taxis in Memphis?

JONES: Da situation such we betta off wit my escort.

SOLOMON: What is this escort?

JONES: Some peepas done threaten my life and my family's. These brothas wanna make sho of safety. Das all. Just our safety.

WILLINS: Someone threatened your life? Who? Can we prove

it was city administration? I hope you kept a record of the threats. We could use that.

JONES: I remembas everything.

WILLINS: We could have a press conference on that alone this afternoon. We gotta do something about the press down here. Good God! They're giving you hell. What's your overall assessment of local press coverage?

JONES: Truth be tole, I don't pay much 'tention to press. Day in the Mayor's pocket, so I don't botha.

SOLOMON: The press has got to be spoonfed. You can't ignore them when you're conducting a public strike. They'll nail ya to the wall. Look, one question I have to ask. Why the hell did ya call a strike in February when garbage don't stink?

JONES: Garbage stink all da time, when you got ta carry it on yo' head.

SOLOMON: Good answer.

WILLINS: Which has nothing to do with the question!

JONES: I answer the question! He axe me...

WILLINS: I heard what he asked you. You've called a strike with no preparation and no backing from the International, and you expect us to just come down here at your personal behest and jump right on in like we're only baking a blueberry pie or something. You're a paid AFSCME organizer, $1000 a month, since 1964. All the training sessions you've been to, you can't remember to call us?

JONES: We called you in '66 when we wanted ta strike.

SOLOMON: And we immediately sent someone to assist you.

JONES: And he tole us, say go back to wuck, obey da coat injunction. Hmph! I got more done dealin' wit the city den yo' man did wit all his runnin' 'roun' and press conferencin'.

SOLOMON: And when our man got back to New York, I fired him for backing down from a mere injunction.

WILLINS: And, the fact is, injunction or no, you all were just as unprepared then as now. It was damned unwise and it jeopardized our plans for...

SOLOMON: Willya lay off, Willins. That's history. Whadda ya gonna do? We got a strike to win and I got an appointment with your Mayor to which I'll be late if your "escorts" don't get here soon. As a matter of fact, I think I'll catch...

JONES: Here dey is now. I tole 'em all 'bout ya'll.

*[SWAHILI, CINNAMON enter in a fast lockstep type of walk. They are wary of SOLOMON because he is white, but they are stiffly polite.]*

SWAHILI: *[Formally to SOLOMON.]* You must be Joshua Solomon and *[Warmly.]* you must be Brotha Craig Willins, the great organizer of the people. Power to the people!

CINNAMON: Powa ta da peepas!

SOLOMON: *[Subtlest saracasm.]* I feel utterly safe! What can I say? Very secure. Can we get to the hotel now?

JONES: *[Sensing, uneasy.]* Sho, we kin do dat.

SOLOMON: *[To JONES as they all exit.]* On the way over fill us in on everything.

*[Lights and Images and Sound cut to a "banquet hall" where suspended are three flags: confederate, U.S. and the state flag of Tennessee We hear a tremendous ovation and see the MAYOR graciously acknowledging the "audience." He stands behind a "garbage-can podium." SOLOMON and WILLINS, wary and bored, watch from the "back" of the hall. As the MAYOR speaks, several times PEOPLE come out and empty kitchen garbage containers or place a garbage can somewhere, adding to the piles. Flashbulbs go off as the MAYOR speaks.]*

MAYOR: I thank you for this most kind honor. I had only

stopped in on my way to a very important meeting and hadn't expected to be acknowledged at this gathering. After all, we're here today to honor Frank, the highly esteemed publisher of what I consider to be the very best newspaper in the South, the *Memphis Scimitar*. Under Frank the *Scimitar* has stood for the very best values the South has to offer, and, I might add, the nation has to offer. Stability, truth, justice, honesty, solid family values. It is only fitting and proper that Frank be honored by the Jewish and Christian Fellowship Society of Memphis. His newspaper has brought more inter-ethnic and inter-faith understanding than any other institution I can think of in this town. Frank and I go a long ways back. The same Alma Mater, same church, same neighborhood, same watering spots.

*[A ripple of polite chuckles from the "audience."]*

I won't dwell on that last reference.

*[More polite chuckles.]*

And I won't take up any more of your time. I would like to acknowledge Joshua Solomon, the international representative of the American Federation of State, County and Municipal Employees, who's come here to meet with me and help me solve an important labor dispute that is occuring as I speak this very moment. Joshua, where are you?

*[SOLOMON half-heartedly raises his hand and accepts very lukewarm applause.]*

Thank you, ladies and gentlemen; I bid you adieu and God bless each and every one of you.

*[Another rousing, long ovation and flashbulbs popping as the MAYOR leaves the area and walks into his office where he meets SOLOMON. The BLUESMAN pushes on a desk that is made of garbage cans. Lights and images shift.]*

SOLOMON: I'm here on behalf of Mr. Jones and his men who work in the sanitation department.

MAYOR: Ah yes, the deranged Mr. Jones.

SOLOMON: You say deranged?

BLUESMAN: He has no sense of responsibility. He came into my office, flashed me, and for no reason struck me.

SOLOMON: Flashed ya? Whaddya mean?

MAYOR: He pulled off his clothes and struck me.

SOLOMON: I don't know what you're talking about. I came because they are members of my union and they've declared a strike.

MAYOR: They are poor, uneducated colored men to whom the city extends an opportunity to earn a living that is on a level with their education, or lack of it.

SOLOMON: I can't believe what I'm hearing.

MAYOR: Those men were riled up by an irresponsible Mr. Jones who has some ignorant political agenda up his sleeve. I want to solve this problem as much as you, but you'd better get your facts straight if you want to help me solve it.

SOLOMON: Let's be frank, Mr. Mayor. I am not here to help you to do anything. I'm here to help a bunch of poor working men salvage a little dignity out of this whole mess. And that seems possible and little enough to accomplish.

MAYOR: In 1956 the distinguished novelist William Faulkner gave the Negroes some solid advice in an essay he called "If I Were a Negro."* He said, "We must learn to deserve equality so that we can hold and keep it after we get it. We must learn responsibility, the responsibility of equality."

SOLOMON: Hey, sounds great, but I'm not a Southern fiction man. I do know that Southern fiction and Southern real-

*Ebony Magazine, September, 1956, pp.70-73

ity get mixed up sometimes. But I never needed a book to tell me that. Maybe one day we'll do literary chitchat over tea. Right now I have another purpose.

MAYOR:  I think I know your purpose, Mr. Solomon.

SOLOMON:  And I think I know yours. I know why you dragged us through that syrupy Christian and Jewish...

MAYOR:  Jewish and Christian...

SOLOMON:  Right. Look, first I think: what is this "Take a Jew to Lunch" bit? I think it's useless. But anyway, that's another story. Then I realize you want me to witness what a great guy they think you are. You smile and preen before the cameras and then come into the lion's den with me.

MAYOR:  I'm hardly what you'd call a lion, Mr. Solomon.

SOLOMON:  Not you, me. Your banquets don't impress me, unless they can deliver formal recognition of the union, union dues checkoff, an immediate wage increase and vastly improved working conditions. That dues checkoff is paramount. We want city payroll to deduct dues directly from the paychecks and give the money to us.

MAYOR:  That wage increase is worth discussing, but the other three are illegal and impossible. This whole thing is beginning to sound like a union ploy to get the men's money. This city has never dealt with unions and never will.

SOLOMON:  Bullshit! Ever since Mayor Crump's administration back in 1909 and even before that—since the Civil War ended—there's been informal recognition of every white union in this town that does any business with the government.

MAYOR:  Congratulations, you've done some homework.

SOLOMON:  Yeah, I did a lotta homework on Memphis and you too.

MAYOR:  Then surely you understand that the Crump administration set the precedent, which is that the city merely generates certain understandings with certain contractors who, in turn, deal with their workers. And if there are ever problems, they are handled through the open door policy that this administration follows. Why, I've done more personally for those men than any other administrator in this city; I...

SOLOMON:   In other words, we can come to the big house on our knees and beg you for favors.

MAYOR:   New Yorkers love the theatre.

SOLOMON:   And there's plenty of it here in Memphis. Mr. Mayor, this strike is not going to go away.

MAYOR:   *[Waving letters.]* And neither is the opposition, Mr. Solomon. I've gotten hundreds of letters supporting my position. Memphis is known as America's cleanest city. We aim to keep it that way. Here's numerous letters from volunteers who've offered to help collect garbage: Jaycees, Boy Scouts, church groups, P.T.A.'s, you name it, even a couple of Negro organizations. I shall not back down from my position!

SOLOMON:   Position? You mean as in prize geshmat? Huh? Best little ole converted Jew this side of the West Bank.

MAYOR:   *[Angry, defensive.]* I don't think you're making any sense now.

SOLOMON:   I'm making all the sense in the world if ya had the sense to see what's really happening in this town. You lost your kishkas *[guts]* and  converted to Episcopalianism.

MAYOR:   That has nothing to do with...

SOLOMON:   It has to do with everything. What are ya, crazy? Or some kind of perverted shlemiel? *[foolish person]* It's one thing for a Jew to convert to Christianity. It's something else for a Jew to convert to redneck posturing. You should know better! You're upholding a system that hates Jews too! You can't be a redneck putz *[evil intentioned person]* without hating Jews, along with the blacks and anybody else who ain't redneck. You wanna get along down here, so you go along with whatever they tell ya. You're a goddam putz is what ya are!

**BLUESMAN:** You have no right to come here telling me how to live my life, what to believe and what to be!

**MAYOR:** If you were from Memphis, you'd understand some very basic things about this place. My family's been here four generations. One learns that there are regional traditions which you may not be astute enough to understand, but which have brought any kind of progress we do have. I was Mayor in 1963, you must have read.

**SOLOMON:** Yeah, I read, and I even read that your wife may be the next queen of the Cotton Festival or something. Great! I'm tickled pink for her. But if you're about to give me any crap about how you personally made everything better for the "uneducated, poor colored" sanitation men, or how your favorite chauffeur is a Negro, spare me.

**MAYOR:** I was about to say that when the question of union recognition came up, the temporarily misguided city council had passed a resolution to recognize the union. The public raised such an outcry that I publically resigned from the mayor's office rather than sign that resolution. And when they changed the form of government to the strong-Mayor/weak council system, I ran again for Mayor and won overwhelmingly. Just a few months ago, as a matter of fact. The people gave me a fresh mandate. I will uphold it. People here do things differently and no Yiddish-speaking, Jewish thug from New York is gonna come here and reorder our ways!

**SOLOMON:** I don't speak Yiddish, I use it when appropriate.

I sure as hell ain't no thug, even though I'm from New York. And I am not Jewish! To be Jewish is to be Jew-like. I am not like a Jew, I am a Jew! And I ain't about to convert to some archaic "ways" of behavior that are an affront to human decency, and I don't mean the Episcopalians. You're a dud, man, a gauleiter at the loading pens. *[Shouting.]* For Chrissake, get it through your head that we consider Memphis our Armageddon of the South!

**MAYOR:** *[Derisive laughter.]* Your Armageddon, indeed! I've got a putz here with grandiose illusions. I should call you General Solomon perhaps?

**SOLOMON:** Listen to this, you smarmy, backwoods Pharoah: Every day. Every day, we'll be out there marching and singing, maybe even dancing when we cross Beale Street— not me, of course. But we'll be out there until doomsday if we hafta. And those people who you think are with you, ain't gonna be so with you when Memphis has its spring awakening. Those magnolias ain't gonna do the trick. And I wanna say one more thing: You're a conceited, racist, geshmat sonuvabitch and your lying tongue is coated with redneck shit!

*[The MAYOR leaps up, enraged as the BLUESMAN loudly hits a discordant chord. Lights and Images shift to the Lorraine Motel, night, where JONES, SWAHILI and CINNAMON heatedly converse. The BLUESMAN sits in a dark corner.]*

**SWAHILI:** You da leader, not Solomon, not Willins, not the NAACP, not the ministers wit all that Jesus talk. We here to back up and protect you, not them.

**CINNAMON:** Right on!

**JONES:** I unnastans dat. But we needs day hep too. You gotta figure dat in.

**SWAHILI:** Help, sure. "Help" is what they 'sposed ta do, not run things. They meeting and strategizing like they running things. We don't take no orders from no whitey. Stokeley Carmichael got that straight. He said BLACK Power, not Negro Power.

CINNAMON:  Right on!

SWAHILI:  Look, mzee, we ready to follow you into battle. We'll give our lives at yo' orders. But we need you to be a strong leader. To keep the black man in control of the black man's destiny.

CINNAMON:  Right on!

JONES:  You don't hafta worry 'bout dat. I know how to keep control.

*[Lights and Images shift to NAACP FIRST SECRETARY's "office" where she talks excitedly with SOLOMON, WILL-INS and MOORE. Before we actually hear them speak MLK'S VOICE speaks. As MLK speaks, the BLUESMAN wanders in and perches on a garbage can.]*

MLK'S VOICE:  "...The masses of people are rising up. And wherever they are assembled today, whether they are in Johannesburg, South Africa; Nairobi, Kenya; Accra, Ghana; New York City; Atlanta, Georgia; Jackson, Mississippi; or Memphis, Tennessee—the cry is always the same—'We want to be free.' "

BLUESMAN:  *[Singing blues fashion.]*

FREE, FREE, FREE, OH LAWD, FREE

BUT WHERE'S THE KEY TO UNLOCK THE CHAINS

WHERE'S THE KEY THAT WILL SET US FREE

SECRETARY:  *[As if answering him.]*  The NAACP is making plans to mount a boycott of downtown businesses which will further pressure the Mayor. We're also issuing a national press release so that we can avoid the local press.

**WILLINS:** That's it? What about funds to help the strikers' families?

**SECRETARY:** That they can't do, but they can ask others to solicit funds as soon as an account is set up.

**WILLINS:** What's wrong with our union accounts? Why are they delaying progress?

**SECRETARY:** We merely feel local agencies should handle relief funds. I wouldn't say we're "delaying progress." That's a real stretch, even for you.

**WILLINS:** Meaning?

**SECRETARY:** Meaning that your pushy condescension toward people down here is a bit much.

**WILLINS:** Pushy? We're the ones being pushed.

**SOLOMON:** Look, what about lawyers from the Defense Fund? Lots of people will be arrested before this is over.

**SECRETARY:** They've promised us three full-time.

**WILLINS:** Three? Three? What are we supposed to do with 'em, crucify 'em or something?

**SOLOMON:** We'll work with the three and, Craig, make a note, have the international send us some additional ones. And, by the way, where's Jones? Wasn't he supposed to be here an hour ago?

**WILLINS:** Maybe he's out declaring another strike.

**MOORE:** Did he call?

**SECRETARY:** No.

**SOLOMON:** This is a heck of way to plan a strike. Let's talk about ministerial support. Rev. Moore, what's the scoop there?

**MOORE:** I've got seven big Negro churches lined up so far. They promise good singing, good preaching and plenty of good fried chicken. Lawd ha'mercy!

**WILLINS:** Amen to that!

**MOORE:** Much as I hate to say it, that mace they sprayed on us at the parade opened up a lot of eyes. A group of ministers formed a group called Community on the Move for Equality, or, COME, for short. I hate that name, but they based it on Isaiah, Chapter One, Verse 18, so I couldn't say anything. Anyway, they've offered to negotiate with the Mayor.

**SOLOMON AND WILLINS:** No way!

**WILLINS:** No group negotiates for the union! We are a striking union, not a civil rights demonstration or a religious revival!

**SECRETARY:** It was an offer, not a demand!

**SOLOMON:** Rev. Moore, you think they'll help us plan strike strategy? Mobilize bodies?

**MOORE:** I'm sure. They said "negotiate" because that's usually a role that Negro clergy play down here.

**WILLINS:** Well, there's no more "down here" or "up there." Some methods just won't do anymore.

**MOORE:** Those COME people have the power to raise lots of money for a strike fund.

**SOLOMON:** Of course, and we welcome whatever they raise. Meanwhile, Craig, take a note: ask all the Federation locals to donate money and food. And ask George Meany to tap the National AFL-CIO. Tell 'im we estimate $15,000 weekly to pull this off. And, by the way, the Sanitation workers are eligible to get food stamps. Put somebody on that.

**MOORE:** You know, there's a chance we could get King down here to help out, maybe lead a march.

**SECRETARY:** I don't think that's a good idea. We could lose our focus on the issues.

**WILLINS:** We could also get national attention focused on Memphis.

**SOLOMON:** As long as the strike remains the central focus, I have no objection to King's coming.

**MOORE:** Well, Rev. Lawson's in that COME group, and he's a personal friend of King.

**WILLINS:** Could you specifically ask Lawson if he'd look into getting King?

**MOORE:** Sure. Any objection to that, Miss Secretary?

**SECRETARY:** No, I'll go along with the group. Let's get King.

*[JONES, SWAHILI, and CINNAMON enter. JONES noticeably swaggers. SWAHILI and CINNAMON act like menacing bodyguards. WILLINS is obviously disgusted with them.]*

**SOLOMON:** I don't understand; did I give you the wrong time for the meeting?

**JONES:** No, you gived da right time, but dere was impo'tent union work had ta be done.

**SOLOMON:** We thought we were doing important union work. What were you doing?

**JONES:** We got us a strike on. Peepas don't get no paydays. Day got to eat. Bertha Wilson over on Hernando got six chilrens not one speck of cornmeal in the house, no milk, no rice or potatoes. Her husband was sick las' week, ain't got but one day's pay. And now he on strike. Day needed food. We collect some money and food and carry it to 'em. But while I'm takin' care of Miss Wilson, long come Shiloh Rankin live over on Grant Street and his son still in jail from the march. Cain't make bail and he gittin' sick 'cause he got da sickle cell, but da police say he fakin'. I hada fine some money and send a few of my mens ta run see about dat. Alright, now we meet back at Retail Clerks Hall and

fidden to come here, den the phone ring. One of our
union men had a fight with some scabs over on Handy
Square at Beale Street. He hurt two a dem and got cut up
fah his troubles and day taken him to the hospital 'mergency. Hospital 'mergency say he got ta pay foe day treat
'im. He ain't got two quartas ta rub tagetha. I run 'round
and got what donations I could and run over to the hospital. Den we stop by here.

**SOLOMON:**  I can't say that ya wasted your time. Everything
ya did was necessary. Okay? But...

**WILLINS:**  Since you collected all that money, and I hope you
kept receipts, couldn't you used one dime of it to call here
and alert us?

**JONES:**  Wudden no time and I didn't know da numba nohow.

**WILLINS:**  *[Mimicking Southern accent.]*  No phonebooks in
Memphis, eh?

**JONES:**  *[Exploding.]*  I ain't got no time ta stop and be studyin'
some phonebook or hustlin' receipts while mah mens is suf-
ferin' and need my help!

**SWAHILI:**  We showed what we been doing. What about ya'll?
Sittin' up here havin' tea?

**MOORE:**  Now, hold on, young man. Everybody been...

**WILLINS:**  We've been organizing an intelligent response to
the events. We've been making plans, noting resources, ana-
lyzing the situation, weighing options, trying to create a
unified approach. That's all!

**SWAHILI:**  While the people perish in the streets!

**WILLINS:**  Not nearly as much as your brain seems to perish
when confronted with sound reason.

**SWAHILI:**  Just 'cause you bring your tired, bourgeois ass from
*UPSOUTH* to Memphis, you think...

WILLINS: Popcorn, man! Damn popcorn! That's all you talk!

SOLOMON: Goddamit, Willins! Look what you're doin'!

MOORE: Gentlemen, we have a lady present. Lawd ha'mercy!

SOLOMON: *[Trying to make peace.]* I apologize for the language, Miss Secretary, Reverend, but not for the sentiment. I was trying to say, our signals got a little crossed, but we all seem to be doing something useful. Bury the hatchet or the Mayor's gonna take a giant, aristocratic crap on all of us!

SECRETARY: *[Taking* SOLOMON's *signal.]* Now that makes sense. T.O., you guys are doing a great job. You just taught me something about what it takes to keep a strike going. I sympathize with Mrs. Wilson.

MOORE: *[A friend.]* Brotha Jones always been just like that. He can't help himself when he sees his men in need.

SWAHILI: *[Blindly.]* Dig dat!

CINNAMON: Right on!

SOLOMON: Okay, that's all understood. Now, we can go on with this meeting. You guys pull up a seat. With your knowledge of what's happening on the streets, we can make even better plans for this...

SWAHILI: The Invaders don't share no knowledge unless we're sure of who we sharing it with. The pig got ghetto listening posts everywhere. It's a sure bet they got the NAACP wired up.

SECRETARY: I can assure you that my office is...

WILLINS: Good God!

MOORE: Perhaps we can share with you what's already been decided.

SWAHILI: How can you make any decisions without the leader? Jones is the leader, understand. This strike is being led by a black warrior. Ya'll have a difficult time accepting that, but that's what happenin'.

**SOLOMON:** This strike is being led by the workers. We are here to serve them in various capacities, and in an organized fashion. Let's get that straight now!

**SWAHILI:** Well, let's do that! That's what Brotha Jones and the rest of us been doing, serving in various capacities. That's elementary! Che Guevara teaches us that...

**WILLINS:** If Jones is the leader, why are you doing all the talking?

**SWAHILI:** I only sought to defend him.

**WILLINS:** Well, he looks capable enough of defending himself. After all, he is the "warrior leader." Mr. Jones, can we go on with the meeting?

**JONES:** We can, but not now.

**SOLOMON:** What's wrong with now? We're trying to get caught up with...

**JONES:** Tomorrow is grocery shopping day. Whole lotta folks out dere ain't gon' have nothin' ta shop with. Right now, I got to make some runs and collect donations, and den I got ta...

**WILLINS:** What are you saying?

**JONES:** I'm 'fficially adjournin' da meetin' 'till foe' o'clock tomorrow when I can be h...

**WILLINS:** Wait!

**SOLOMON:** *[To Willins.]* No! Don't start.

**SECRETARY:** T.O., we can't let that much time elapse with nothing done.

**MOORE:** Brotha Jones, let me explain; we...

**JONES:** Ain't no 'splainin', Brotha Moe. Cain't be done no otha way. I got too much on my plate now. Let me take care of those otha mattas first, den I kin tell mah plan. Ya'll kin hep me work out da mechanics.

SWAHILI: *[Subtle threat.]* For the record, the Invaders completely back Mzee Jones on this decision to adjourn.

SOLOMON: Fine! Meeting adjourned. Why don't you guys run along now?

JONES: Thank you, fah dat respeck. Brotha Moe, would you like to come along wit us and help collect donations?

MOORE: Uh, not tonight, but, uh, I got collection plates goin' 'round my congregation on Sunday.

SOLOMON: I'll check in with you early in the morning, okay?

JONES: Fine wit me. Let's move out.

*[JONES exits, followed by SWAHILI and CINNAMON who salute at the "door" as they leave.]*

SWAHILI: Power to the People!

CINNAMON: Powa ta da Peepas!

SOLOMON: Reverend Moore, you know T.O. better than any of us. What's going on?

MOORE: Jones is basically a good man with a big dream. Sometimes a person's dream is the highest achievement in his life. You get my drift?

SOLOMON: *[To Willins.]* I think I do. But Jones seems like he's in the grip of a potential nightmare. Neo-Stalinists. It's like the Stalinists have returned in a different guise. I used to have regular fistfights with Stalinists all over Brooklyn. In the 40's. I can't go through that again.

WILLINS: The age of fists is over. But we still have to fight them, and we have to win, some kinda way, and I think we will. *[Commanding tone.]* Let me handle this problem, Josh, okay?

BLUESMAN: *[Singing as before while lights fade.]*

FREE FREE FREE, OH LAWD FREE
BUT WHERE'S THE KEY TO UNLOCK THE CHAINS
WHERE'S THE KEY THAT WILL SET US FREE

*[Lights and Images shift to a "meeting room" in City Hall. The* MAYOR, POLICE CHIEF, SOLICITOR, *and the* COLLABORATOR *in shadows. It is several days later.]*

**MLK'S VOICE:** "...It is no longer a choice between violence and nonviolence in this world; it's nonviolence or nonexistence..."

**COLLABORATOR:** We don't see the Invaders as much of a problem; we have several infiltrators keeping on eye on them. Rev. Lawson is now the principal strategist for the daily marches. FBI says he's a pinko.

**SOLICITOR:** How did the FBI get involved in this?

**CHIEF:** I called them for background information; Among other things Lawson's a coward. He was jailed for refusing to serve in Vietnam, and he's one of King's cohorts. That Solomon guy was a member of the Young Peoples' Socialist League. And Mr. Jones is merely an ex-poolhall hustler, an eighth grade dropout, a rakish buffoon who possesses a crude shrewdness. We may be able to use all that.

**SOLICITOR:** For what?

**MAYOR:** For the wellbeing of our city, of course!

**SOLICITOR:** How about just negotiating a settlement of the strike? Did the FBI tell you how to do that?

**MAYOR:** Continue.

**POLICE CHIEF:** Is there any chance they'll try to get King down here?

**COLLABORATOR:** A good chance. They want King to lead a march.

**MAYOR:** Mr. Solicitor, you will prepare an injunction against that march.

SOLICITOR:  The whole thing is escalating because we're not facing some facts. All of us know that those men deserve some kinda raise, some kinda simple consideration, which could...

MAYOR:  I'd rather have our meeting after the agent has finished.

SOLICITOR:  Bunk the formalities!

MAYOR:  This is the MAYOR'S Advisory Board.

SOLICITOR:  I don't give a damn whose advisory board it is; I'm on it by law, and I'm an elected representative of all the people like you. I have the responsibility to advise the Mayor, even if he's too bullheaded to accept honest advice! Injunctions past and present are virtually useless in these kinds of situations. Might as well as get an injunction to stop the Mississippi River from flooding. Fact: The union is not going to go away. Fact: They're mobilizing much of this town and galvanizing national support. Fact: In '60 and '61 boycotters managed to practically close down the main shopping districts. Why this confrontation? Let's be flexible and save ourselves a lot of headache.

MAYOR:  So, you'd get rid of a headache by chopping off your head? This city cannot appear to cave in to demands from any union. We'd be bankrupt in three years. We'd look like New York.

SOLICITOR:  You exaggerate! Look, the blacks have been here ever since there was a Memphis and it behooves us to...

MAYOR:  To placate Jones and his ilk without outside influence. Memphis belongs to Memphians. We can resolve our own problems without carpetbagging agitators. I have a plan in process now. But it takes time.

*[Lights and Images shift to the mayor's office where* JONES

*awaits the* MAYOR. *The* BLUESMAN *leads in the* MAYOR *and* POLICE CHIEF.*]*

**MLK'S VOICE:** "...let us keep the issues where they are. The issue is injustice. The issue is the refusal of Memphis to be fair and honest in its dealings with its public servants, who happen to be sanitation workers..."

**MAYOR:** You're early, Mr. Jones.

**JONES:** Dat's 'cause I want to settle dis strike soon. And I hope dis ain't no tricknology wit da Pole-lease here and everything.

**MAYOR:** Absolutely not! I can assure you. The Chief is here officially as a member of my Advisory Board. You can walk out of here anytime you like.

**JONES:** I stay fah now. But let me be clear: I'm heah on da men's behalf. It ain't got ta do wit' no special favors fah me. It's da mens need hep like I tried ta tell ya in the fust place back in early February. Here it is, March fixin' to close off and we still scufflin'. If you took the time to listen to me, none of this mess woulda happen.

**MAYOR:** Fine. I'm ready to listen now, but are you? Last time we spoke you said you do the authorizing among your men, is that not so?

**JONES:** Dat's so.

**MAYOR:** Why, then, have others begun calling the shots?

**JONES:** Who you speakin' of?

**MAYOR:** No games, Jones. Solomon, Lawson, the NAACP, the ministers. I thought I was dealing with one man, you. Now, I understand that Martin King is coming to lead one of Lawson's marches.

**JONES:** *[Standing.]* King? Who said that?

**CHIEF:** That Willins fella got a police permit for a special march. Says King is supposed to lead it.

JONES: Willins?

MAYOR: Didn't you help plan the march?

JONES: *[Raging.]* I don't know nothin' 'bout no King comin' here! I didn't authorize that.

MAYOR: Just as I suspected, which means that you don't control things anymore, or at least you won't when King gets here.

JONES: Bullshit! Dey can't do nothin' witout da mens and dat's me. That damn Willins went behine mah back!

MAYOR: *[Pressing his case.]* Indeed he did. And that Solomon fellow strikes me as a man who would milk his neighbor's cow through the fence.

JONES: Maybe, at las' we agree on something.

MAYOR: Sit please. I'll speak plainly to you, because I can tell you're a man who appreciates the truth and who has an intelligent grasp on reality: I've reconsidered. I think we can sit down and balance things out, so no one loses everything, and everyone wins something. But I want to talk directly to the boss, and that's you, I think.

JONES: *[Preening.]* Oh, it's me all right. You can ass any of the mens about dat. I come to talk man to man, like in the old days. I'll settle this strike myself!

MAYOR: *[Gleefully.]* Good! Let's talk, man to man. You told me what you want, let me tell you what I want.

*[The BLUESMAN frowns at JONES and turns his back and walks directly into the next scene where he sits scowling. Lights and Images shift to home of the SECRETARY where she talks animatedly with MOORE and WILLINS. It is now March 20. Projected headlines show that King is coming to lead the March.]*

MOORE:   The National Guard, the sheriff, state highway patrol and every policeman in the city will be on duty that day. Lawd ha'mercy!

WILLINS:   Don't fret. Memphis doesn't want bad press. And Lawson's got the rowdy element under control. Guaranteed peace on March 28th.

*[Enter a swaggering JONES, wearing dark glasses, SWAHILI and CINNAMON. The latter two stand "guard" behind JONES.]*

JONES:   *[to SWAHILI and CINNAMON.]* At ease. *[To the Others.]* Sorry I'm late. I come here ta tell ya'll da march is cancelled.

WILLINS:   *[Laughing derisively, incredulously.]* Oh yeah, who cancelled it?

JONES:   Me! Things got outta hand. Ya'll got King comin' ta march, but afta King go away we got the same garbage lef'. I respeck King very much, he done a lot fah our peepas, but ya'll shoulda cleared bringin' in King with the local first. Ain't nobody listenin' to da sanitation mens.

WILLINS:   The whole thing is about the sanitation men.

SECRETARY:   T.O., we listened to the sanitation men; that's why we're here.

JONES:   Brotha Moe here been wit me befoe any of ya'll. He know what I'm talkin' 'bout. 'Bout da onliest thing the sanitation men doin' now is providin' bodies fah da daily march.

MOORE:   But, I honestly think that King's presence will do more good than harm for the strike.

JONES:   It ain't 'bout that, Brotha Moe. Can't no Messiah hep us unless da Messiah is one of us. King comes and King goes, but what happens when he gone? If we wants things ta change, we gotta change dem. If peepas cain't save they-

sef, ain't no savin' gon' happen. We don't need no civil rights
march, much as we needs a strike settlement.

WILLINS:  Man, are you cra...

MOORE:  *[Rapidly.]*  Brotha Jones, the sanitation men are poor
and King is running a Poor People's Campaign, because
if you're poor, you don't have any civil rights or labor
rights that most people respect. That's why...

JONES:  I knowed dat, Rev. Moore. But I'm talkin' 'bout leadership decisions. I made my decision. I'm givin' orders to
cancel da march.

SECRETARY:  That's stupid!

WILLINS:  You can't stop the march!

JONES:  I can if I declare da strike ova and tell da mens not ta
march.

WILLINS:  Declare the strike over? What a bumbling, inept,
simple...

MOORE:  *[Desperate as a friend.]*  T.O., do you know something
we don't know? Solomon's in the negotiating session with
the mediation board now. Did they reach an agreement?

JONES:  Not far as I know, but since the mens ain't present,
any agreement is something we ain't agreed to.

SECRETARY:  I think you better take stock of what you're saying. Think, T.O., think!

MOORE:  Have you figured out some way to settle this thing
without the march?

JONES:  I have a way. I been talkin' to top peepas.

WILLINS:  "Top peepas?" Is this a new race of human beings,
these "top peepas?"

JONES:  Da Mayor included.

WILLINS:  You talked to the Mayor? When?

JONES:  A while ago. Been talkin'. Dere are better ways ta settle dis strike and da impo'tent people involved need ta throw day ideas on the table.

**WILLINS:** You've been talking to the Mayor behind our backs. Making your own deals? Is that it?

**JONES:** It's our own strike, ain't it?

**WILLINS:** You ignorant damn fool!

**SWAHILI:** Don't disrespect our leader like that!

**WILLINS:** And you're just a simple-minded nigga!

**MOORE:** Maybe if we'd just listen to what he has to say, we could fix this.

**JONES:** Ain't no fixin', it's through. I'm calling my mens off the streets.

**WILLINS:** If you try to do something like that... Can't you understand that if union labor loses in Memphis, it loses the South. The union is in this for blood. We're not going to let you destroy us! You and these nappy nignogs can go to hell. You're through in this strike. I'll see that you're fired before nightfall.

**SWAHILI:** Little sucker ass oreo nigga. You the principal reason why black people been wallowing in America's pigslop. You went to some white man's school and learned two/three big words and think you can lead the people. You was sent here by Charley to cool the niggas out with marching and singing, to stop the people's revolution. You the enemy! My leader has declared the strike ended.

**WILLINS:** Leader? He couldn't lead ducks to a pond in the Sahara desert. Revolution? The only revolution you people ever made was with circular rhetoric. You can't even organize a strike, much less a revolution. Go organize your miserably ignorant life! *[Laughing sarcastically.]* Revolutionaries!? What is that, a new TV gameshow? I ain't got nothin' for a ignorant chittlin chewer.

SWAHILI: *[Whipping out his sawed off shotgun.]* What you got for this? Huh?

SECRETARY: Stop this! Please God!

MOORE: Ain't no need for that, Swahili.

JONES: *[Also fearful.]* At ease, Swa...

SWAHILI: *[Beyond listening.]* Shut up, alla ya'll. *[To Willins.]* Oh, you quiet now, ain'tcha?

WILLINS: I'm quiet 'cause I'm amazed at how far a nigga will go to prove he's a revolutionary. You wanna kill me, Mr. Swahili. Here. *[Rips open his shirt and exposes his bare flesh.]* Show the world how a brave black revolutionary can kill another black man. Show what it took for a black man to kill Malcom X! Kill me! Kill me! Go ahead! Maybe the crackers'll give you a medal for killing another nigga. Kill me, nigga!

JONES: *[Clearly pleading.]* We don't need no moe of dem, let's move out.

*[A tense pause after which SWAHILI puts his gun away. Even CINNAMON breathes a sigh of relief. As the BLUESMAN plays a sorrowful sounding few notes, JONES, SWAHILI and CINNAMON depart. Lights and Images shift to the Lorraine Motel, JONES' room, late evening. JONES is having a drink. WILLINS enters. The BLUESMAN sits in a dark corner.]*

WILLINS: I don't know why you asked me over, but I'm glad you did; I wanted to talk privately with you too.

JONES: Pull up a chair, have a drink.

WILLINS: Tennessee corn. That's illegal.

JONES: And good too!

WILLINS: I'll have one, thanks. Why'd you ask me over and, by the way, where's your dogs?

**JONES:**  Day run off to a meetin'. I ask you ova to apologize for what happened this afternoon. I ain't neva intended fah none a dat.

**WILLINS:**  *[Sincerely.]* I know. I know. And I apologize for what I said. Anger, man, just anger.

**JONES:**  Day call dayself protectin' me 'cause I got threats on my life, quite a few. I'm scared. Das all. Just plain scared.

**WILLINS:**  Well, so am I.

**JONES:**  You didn't act scared!

**WILLINS:**  I'm scared for the movement, the union, the strike, this whole damn country, things like that. What you said about calling off the strike scared me.

**JONES:**  I didn't mean fah it ta do dat. It's how I truly feel; it's what I got ta do fah da wellbein' of da mens.

**WILLINS:**  Well, I have to do something for the wellbeing of the movement.

**JONES:**  Yeah?

**WILLINS:**  *[Pulling out papers with figures.]* Jones, the records say you collected and disbursed something like seven thousand dollars over the last month. We don't have enough receipts to account for one tenth of that. The executive board is concerned about allegations of theft. What happened to that money?

**JONES:**  I didn't steal no money!

**WILLINS:**  These are the statements of institutional donors. Each one shows what they raised and have given to the relief fund through you. These are the receipts for some of that money, and this is the figure that shows the amount of money unaccounted for from you. It looks like stealing.

**JONES:**  I didn't steal no money! Who said I stolt it?

**WILLINS:**  No one, yet. But imagine what would happen if this got out. The IRS, the press, the courts—they'd all get involved. The strike fails, the union is busted and you get indicted and go to prison. And the press has the freedom to fan the flames. I've spoken to several lawyers about this and they all agree that such things could happen if this got out.

JONES:   But I didn't steal no money is what I'm tryin' ta tell ya. Why would I do dat now, afta all dese years of struggle? I ain't never done nothin' like dat wit money dat belong ta da union.

WILLINS:   I don't have a personal judgement in the matter; I think you're an honest man; I'm talking about others, especially the men. They'd be buried up under a mountain of public relations garbage. Nowadays, it's the appearance, not the fact that counts.

JONES:   Fah da record I didn't steal no money, but I see yo' point. Is somebody tryin' ta put da word on da streets?

WILLINS:   Not yet. I'll be frank. There's only a few of us who know. We don't want anything to happen to the movement or to you, but...

JONES:   But what?

WILLINS:   In America when you want someone to do something for you, it costs. When you want someone to do nothing for you, it costs. If you declare the strike over, you're gonna make some people mighty angry. So angry, I couldn't stop them from releasing that information to the national press.

JONES:   "Oh, I see," said da blind man. You really wantin' me ta give up leadership of my union.

WILLINS:   *[Folding up his papers.]* No, on the contrary, I want you to be a brave leader of your union. I want you to save it. The deal is this: You can still be president and keep your

salary and come to all the meetings, but you have to follow the international's leadership. And no more private talks
with the Mayor!

JONES: *[Bitterly.]* You been tryin' ta git me eva since you got
here.

WILLINS: Me get you? You got yourself, my brother. You got
yourself when you dumbly called a garbage strike in the
winter without any preparation or backing, when you
improvised a march that left many people injured and in
jail, when you attached yourself to those Invaders from the
black power planet. They're great! They protect you by
threatening to kill me, who came here to serve the union.
We are not making you an offer, Jones.

JONES: Why you do dis? I'm just a man like you. Why you
instead of me? I built a house. I built a house witout yo'
hep. And now heah you come movin' in.

WILLINS: You brought the materials together, but we're build-
ing the house. And it won't be some plantation shanty. T.O.,
you need the right tools to build a strong house. We have
those tools. You don't.

JONES: Hmph! Ya'll ain't built nothin' in the South with dem
tools. We started something and brung you down. Da
whole country heah now because we taken action. And dis
happen 'foe ya'll come.

WILLINS: Even when I use your metaphors I can't make you
understand.

JONES: Don't throw that metashit in my face! You da high and
mighty. You use da white man's talk good as he do. But what
do all dat talk mean? Huh? It mean you kin kill a man like
me, kin kill a whole country fulla peepas, and all you got
ta do is explain it real pretty, and turn it into whatever yo'
words sound like. You talk shit, but you make it smell sweet.

**WILLINS:** You talk some pretty good dudu yourself. I've had my say. You can take it or leave it. What's the word, mzee?

**JONES:** "Take it or leave it." Dat's a lie! You a lie!

**WILLINS:** What? I'm a...

**JONES:** You a lie 'cause you ain't give no choice.

**WILLINS:** You can't understand what I'm saying, can you?

**JONES:** *[Shouting.]* I stood up for those mens when nobody else did!

**WILLINS:** *[Shouting back.]* Well now you gon' hafta sit down for them! Cause that's what they need. Can you understand that?

*[JONES sighs in heavy frustration, nods "yes," pours himself another drink, drinks it down, stares off into space. WILLINS smiles in victory.]*

*[Lights and Images shift to a late night street in Memphis. CIN-NAMON, wearing sandals, walks alone. Revolving red lights, as in a police car, suddenly flash across his body. TWO POLICE-MEN, one white and one black, step into CINNAMON's path.]*

**WHITE POLICEMAN (WP):** *[Mimicking.]* "Powa ta da Peepas," Brother Cinnamon.

**CINNAMON:** What ya'll want?

*[They grab and disarm him.]*

**WP:** Whatsamatter, havin' a spat with the wife?

**CINNAMON:** What is dis about?

**BP:** *[Holding up shotgun.]* This heah is about life on the chain-gang, boy. But those sandals sure are pretty. What are they, from Africa?

**WP:** That's where you shoulda stayed, if you don't like the good ole USA.

*[They begin beating him. He tries in vain to fight back. He is quickly beaten into semi-conciousness.]*

**WP:**  Hold him up straight. Chief of Police sent you this message:

*[The* WHITE POLICEMAN *bangs the shotgun butt down repeatedly on* CINNAMON's *toes.* CINNAMON *screams in agony. Lights, Images and Sound shift to scenes of violence and mayhem taken from photos and recordings of the March 28, 1968 march. We should see examples of looting, beatings, brick throwing, cops shooting, cops arresting, National Guardsmen, fearful looks, fires burning, smoke billowing, mob hysteria.* SOUNDS *are screams, gunshots, tear gas canisters exploding, shouts, running feet, breaking glass, sirens, grief-stricken cries, frenzied traffic and police whistles. Discordant blues sounds filter through it all.* LOCAL NEWSPAPER HEADLINES *from March 28 & 29, 1968 are projected, particularly those that say MLK ran because he was afraid. Lights and Images cut to the* SECRETARY's *office where* SOLOMON, MOORE, WILLINS, *and* JONES *meet.* JONES *is sullen, sulks in a corner. The* BLUESMAN *sympathetically watches* JONES.*]*

**MLK'S VOICE:**  "Now we're going to march again, and we've got to march again, in order to put the issue where it is supposed to be... Somehow, the preacher must say with Jesus, "The spirit of the Lord is upon me, because he hath anointed me to deal with the problems of the poor...""

**SOLOMON:**  Another march? Are you certain this is the best way?

**SECRETARY:**  No choice.

**WILLINS:**  King's people were humiliated. If he can't lead a nonviolent march in Memphis, his entire movement is dead.

**MOORE:**  Not to mention his poor people's march on Washington next month.

**SOLOMON:**  All true, but still another march in Memphis right now is suicidal.

JONES:  Shouldna had no march in the first place!

SOLOMON:  I realize you feel that way, but...

JONES:  Whole lot moe den me feel dat way.

SECRETARY:  But they marched nonetheless. Almost all of the sanitation men.

JONES:  Day was tole day had ta.

SOLOMON:  Okay, let's get back to business. When is the next march planned?

MOORE:  Rev. Lawson said April 8th. He got a commitment from King himself.

SOLOMON:  Six days? Oy vey! Well, if it has to be, it has to be, but we need to...

SECRETARY:  To assure the peace. T.O., you know the men best, and you know the street. Can you talk to those people?

JONES:  What fah?

MOORE:  The mayor's got a army parked outside Memphis. All they need is one excuse for butchery.

JONES:  If nobody march, da army stay put.

WILLINS:  Well, another march will happen, and, this time, we gotta make sure it works. None of us has a choice, you understand, T.O.?

SOLOMON:  He's right, T.O.. We need your help. You've got to spread the word to your men. No violence this time.

JONES:  Mah mens didn't bring no violence, I'm tryin' ta tell ya! I don't know how violence come! Nobody seem to know just who started what and why! That's the word on the street.

SECRETARY:  Yes, T.O., I understand, but maybe they could help stem the violence this time. We'll need lots of parade marshalls.

MOORE:  Right! Invaders could help set an example for peace

by being parade marshalls. Rev. Lawson could train them in the techniques of nonviolence. Can you do that, T.O.?

WILLINS: *[A challenge.]* You mean does T.O. have anymore influence over them?

SOLOMON: It would save lives and it would keep the media's focus on the strike, not on violence. Will you do that, T.O.?

JONES: *[Insecure behind this boast.]* Dey still listen to me. All right, you want parade marshalls, you got parade marshalls!

*[Lights and Images cut to JONES' room at the Lorraine. We hear SWAHILI shout out as soon as the lights shift to him.]*

SWAHILI: Nigga, is you crazy? You want us to be what? Parade marshalls?

*[JONES enters. The BLUESMAN sits in a corner.]*

JONES: Since ya'll protectin' me, I...

SWAHILI: Dig this, we thought we was protectin' the leader. But lately something else happenin'. The ministers negotiating, organizing, giving press conferences. That honky from New York and his number one field nigga running the union, telling the men what to do and when, and the men doing what they told. Ain't paying you no mind. The NAACP and Boy Wilkins gettin' all the play in the national press along with Martin Luther King. King shoulda been glad he was leading a army instead of a buncha lay-down-in-the-street-and-kick-me-niggas! And he comin' back to try again! Why the niggas always got to be the ones being peaceful? When whitey get mad at other whiteys, or anybody else, he go to war. Look what he doin' right now in Vietnam! But he pay the "knee-e-e-e-egro-o-o-oes" to let him roll some tanks over them. The pigs making plans to kill black people right now! The FBI got prisons set up for the rest of us. With uniforms and everything ready. And you want us to march the people right down to the slaughterhouse. Peacefully! No way! No way the Invaders gon' lay down and die peacefully, you dig? Next week we planning on roast pig! It's time to resist by any means necessary like Malcom X say.

JONES: Ya'll want to lead the black race, but when I offer you responsible leadership, you ton it down.

SWAHILI: Leading black people to their slaughter is not responsible leadership! You be the Christian that get eat up in the stadium, not me!

JONES: You afraid.

SWAHILI: Afraid? You right. I'm afraid of being helpless in the face of whitey's brutality. You oughtta see Brotha Cinnamon's feet, what's left of them.

JONES: You cain't stop dat kinda of brutality wit mo' brutality. You afraid Rev. Lawson an' dem is right. You afraid of the power of nunviolence.

SWAHILI: You ever try to stop a wild dog with nonviolence? Naw, nonviolence ain't got enough power to stop these barbaric crackers from stomping your black ass in the ground, unnastan?

JONES: Ya'll oughtta 'least speak ta Rev. Lawson, see what he say.

SWAHILI: Hmmmph! Another reverend, anotha darky preacha officiating over the Negro community! I...

JONES: Anotha man tryin' ta keep peepas from bein' hurt. Da onliest things those men ever wanted were safety and moe pay, better conditions.

SWAHILI: I...

JONES: And ya'll fixin' ta take day safety away. Day garbage men, not warriors. Day collects garbage, not guns. I don't want my mens hurt behine no foolishness. You betta go talk to Lawson. I ain't 'llowin' my mens to go violent.

SWAHILI: Your "mens?" You ain't got no "mens" no more. They don't listen to you. You layed down and got run over. Matta of fact, the street sayin' somebody payin' you to keep quiet. You a useless pile of shit!

[JONES *tries to grab* SWAHILI *who easily avoids him and whips out his gun which he points at* JONES *who stops.*]

SWAHILI:    Don't even think about it, mzee! Your life ain't even at risk anymore. Don't nobody need you! If you died tomorrow, it wouldn't make any difference to what's going on in Memphis; the strike, the union, nothing!

[*The* BLUESMAN *strums a low, funky blues as the Lights and Images shift to a Beale St. Bar which he enters.* JONES *shortly stumbles in, now drunk. He, bottle in hand, stands swaying before the* BLUESMAN. *He begins dancing, slowly, dancing out of sorrow. The song's refrain goes as follows:*]

BLUESMAN:    THE GRAVEDIGGER IS YO' VERY BEST FRIEND.

THE GRAVEDIGGER IS YO' VERY BEST FRIEND

HE ONLY LET YOU DOWN ONCE NO MATTER WHAT YOU BEEN

[JONES *stops dancing, angrily hurls the bottle which breaks offstage. He speaks to no one in particular the following over the background instrumental accompaniment of the* BLUES-MAN:]

JONES:    When I was toting garbage, I knowed every alcoholic in town, da ones live in da shacks and da ones what living high in the big houses. I knowed who was creepin' 'round some back doe on day husband or wife. I knowed who was taking high price drugstore drugs and street drugs. I run to da back of da house ta git da garbage and I seed all kinda womens in the window. Naked! Not a stitch on! Justa lookin' down at ole stinkin', black, empty-face me, and smilin' real big. I seed big, impo'tent men in dis town beatin' on soft, little white womens in da back bedrooms. I heard dem womens scream and beg for mercy. I once seed a father touchin' his near 'bout growed up daughter, touchin' her where no fatha 'sposed ta touch his daughter. One time I pulled a dead baby from the garbage, a little white baby, just born, blood still fresh. Somebody throwed it in the garbage behine a big fine mansion. And peepas treat me like I stink. Nothin' stink worse den da garbage dat da garbage man leave behine everyday.

*[JONES staggers out. The music continues for a short moment until it fades to silence as Lights and Images shift to City Hall where the MAYOR, SOLICITOR and CHIEF listen to the COLLABORATOR. We see headlines that say the courts will allow the second march to happen.]*

**COLLABORATOR:** King'll be staying in the Lorraine Motel, room 306, overlooking Mulberry St. He'll be there through April 8.

**SOLICITOR:** Why do we have to know what room?

**CHIEF:** Security. His security.

**MAYOR:** If someone's after him, it's better they don't get him in Memphis.

**CHIEF:** Did you find out anything more about those Invaders?

**COLLABORATOR:** Only that they been buying guns in Arkansas and that they had something to do with the robbery of that gun store on the west side the other night. We also followed one of them and observed him buying every copy of the *New York Times* he could find. Kinda unusual; something suspicious about that.

**CHIEF:** You're dismissed.

**MAYOR:** Mr. Solicitor, are you sure you've exhausted every legal means to stop another march?

**SOLICITOR:** I told you weeks ago that legally no legitimate public demonstration can be blocked in a country where you have freedom of speech, assembly and petition. Injunction or no, they would march. What's the p...

**MAYOR:** But I don't feel you used every means at your disposal.

**SOLICITOR:** Maybe you'd like to argue the case yourself.

**MAYOR:** Your misguided liberal notions may cost several millions in property damage and a few lives. Did you think of that?

**SOLICITOR:** We can't resist the inevitable. We're dealing with an entire community that wants change, not just a union. It's a new South; it's a new world, a world that we don't own anymore. We need to acquire the grace to accept that new world. My wife is going to march with them.

**MAYOR:** Well, I certainly hope she has proper protection because I think things are going to get out of hand once more.

**SOLICITOR:** She'll have proper protection. Me. I'll be there with her.

**MAYOR:** I see! Throwing away a good career in city government?

**SOLICITOR:** No, Mr. Mayor. I'm starting a good career in city government.

**MAYOR:** *[Boiling.]* Chief?

**CHIEF:** We interrogated that Cinnamon fella the other night, and we feel certain that there's gonna be violence, so every available officer will be on duty, along with sheriff's deputies, state highway patrolmen and almost six thousand National Guard troops with tanks.

MAYOR: Fine. No matter what happens, the decent citizens of Memphis will be protected.

*[A clap of thunder resounds and we hear a rainstorm raging as if outside. Lights, Sounds and Images shift to a collage of MLK activities. The projected images include those of his working amidst the poverty and despair among urban and rural Southern blacks. The activities will highlight the span of his national career as an advocate of civil rights, world peace and poor people in one minute. Excerpts from his final speech are heard shortly after the images have begun. We should hear sounds from the audiences that listened to his speech on April 3, and we should hear the thunder and lightning crashes of the torrential storm that ocurred that night as he spoke at Mason Temple.]*

MLK'S VOICE: "Well, I don't know what will happen now. We've got some difficult days ahead. But it doesn't matter with me now. Because I've been to the mountaintop. And I don't mind. Like anybody, I would like to live a long life. Longevity has its place. But I'm not concerned about that now. I just want to do God's will. And He's allowed me to go up to the mountain. And I've looked over. And I've seen the promised land. I may not get there with you. But I want you to know tonight, that we, as a people will get to the promised land. And I'm happy, tonight. I'm not worried about anything. I'm not fearing any man. Mine eyes have seen the glory of the coming of the Lord."

*[As the images fade, lights rise slowly on JONES in his hotel room the night of April 4, just before the murder of MLK. He is alone, holds a glass in one hand. Nearby is a bottle. Sounds from the street outside enter. We hear VOICES singing nearby. They are singing "Precious Lord, Take My Hand" It is the Operation Breadbasket Band and several ministers who were practicing upstairs at the Lorraine just before King's murder. The BLUESMAN randomly strums along with them. The*

*phone rings in* JONES' *room. Lights fade up on* ALICE MAE *in another area.* JONES *answers.* MUSIC *continues low under the voices of* JONES *and* ALICE MAE.]

JONES: Hello.

ALICE: Ollie?

JONES: None otha.

ALICE: What's wrong witchu?

JONES: Ain't nothin' wrong no moe.

ALICE: You been drinkin'. Somethin' botherin' you, Ollie. You kin talk to me if you feel like it; you know that.

JONES: Right now, ain't nothin' botherin' me.

ALICE: You worried about the march on the eighth?

JONES: I ain't got nothin' ta do wit dat march.

ALICE: You gon' march wit King?

JONES: I reckon everybody marchin', but it don't make no difference.

ALICE: I see you feelin' real good this evenin'. Did you catch his speech?

JONES: I caught it on the radio. Dat man sho make good speeches. He talk so fine, he could talk the sweetness out a pecan pie. Reckon dat what it take nowadays. Pretty talk! He talk real good.

ALICE: Well, that oughtta make ya uplift or somethin'.

JONES: Alice Mae, why you callin' me?

ALICE: You should be callin' me. It's April fourth and I ain't seen one dime from you. You got paid on the first.

JONES: Yo money comin'; don't start wit no worriation. I ain't got time ta hear dat now.

ALICE: I think you betta fine some time to hear what I'm sayin'!

JONES: Right now I'm just flusterated, okay? Call me tomorrow.

ALICE:  You gon' be worse than flusterated if I have to march down to family court and git dat judge ta snatch yo' paycheck. Rent got ta be paid, chilrens need shoes, got ta git groceries, strike or no strike. Don't let me have ta do no marchin'. You betta take the time ta rememba dat!

*[She hangs up. Lights to black on her.* JONES *slowly hangs up.* FRIENDLY YELLING VOICES *emanate from outside the windows. Images are photos of MLK taken during his many marches and crusades.]*

VOICE 1:  Ya'll ain't ready yet? What kinda preachers come late for dinner?

VOICE 2:  Hungry preachers.

VOICE 1:  If ya'll don't get down here to the parking lot in five minutes, I'll have to flunk you. You know what that means.

VOICE 2:  What it mean?

VOICE 1:  No hot cornbread with the collard greens.

VOICE 3:  Rev., you need to stop threatening us poor colored preachers. Yo' wife so pretty, I had to stop and put on some cologne.

VOICE 1:  My wife ain't gonna act pretty ya'll mess up her dinner. She been cooking all day. Fried chicken, greens, candied yams, roast beef, slaw, potato salad, macaroni and cheese, ham, stringbeans, yellow squash, smothered turkey wings, custard pie...

VOICE 2:  Lawd ha'mercy! Keep the motor running.

VOICE 3:  Martin Luther King can't eat none of that; he too fat. Can't even button his shirt he bought last month. Call yo' wife and tell her, say make a lettuce salad for Rev. King.

VOICE 2:  I am a lamb of the Lord, but I cain't eat like one. If he keep talking that way, this boy gon' lose his license to preach.

VOICE 1: Rev. King, better bring a coat; it's getting cool out here.

VOICE 2: Say what?

VOICE 1: I said, it's getting cold and...

*[The explosion of rifle fire cuts short his remarks. JONES leaps up, alert. There is a moment of silence. Suddenly a cacophony of voices is heard. Screams, shouts, cries, running feet, etc.]*

VOICE 1: Martin's been shot! They shot Martin!

VOICE 4: Everybody take cover.

VOICE 3: Get a ambulance. Call a ambulance.

*[JONES drops his drink and starts to run to the door, but he stops short in fear. He barricades the "door" shut with any available garbage. He sits in stunned disbelief and fear as the sounds of mayhem continue and images of King's death and its immediate aftermath are projected. There are the headlines, the photos of the body (if available), the riots, the fires burning, looting, glass breaking, the sound of more gunshots, and the general crowd hysteria that accompanied this event. The SOUNDS fade to silence as the IMAGES continue for the duration of "Precious Lord" as sung by the BLUESMAN. As he sings, the surrounding images slowly change to those of the funeral in Atlanta, the general mourning throughout the country. This includes news headlines and photos. The last set of headlines and photos should be the announcement that the strike is settled. Time has passed during this scene and we understand that it is now April 16, evening, as the BLUESMAN finishes the song and retires to a corner. Images return to stills of the external Lorraine Motel. MOORE pushes the garbage aside and enters, a black ribbon pinned to his lapel. JONES barely acknowledges him.]*

MOORE: It's over, T.O., it's over.

*[Silence.]*

Did you hear me? I said, it's over.

*[Pause.]*

JONES:  What's over?

MOORE:  The strike, man! Lawd ha'mercy! The strike over. You won. You listening? You won!

JONES:  Naw, Brotha Moe, I ain't won. I loss. I loss. And you know dis' 'cause you watched me lose. I loss everything. Even King's life. It's like I killed him, pulled the trigger. He come ta hep us and he died. If I'da kept him outta here, he'd be alive. I loss, Brotha Moe. I ain't blamin' nobody but me. Cain't blame nobody but me.

MOORE:  I been knowing you for over 20 years, and I ain't never heard you sound this sorry for yourself. It's time to celebrate now.

JONES:  Eight cents a hour! They got eight cents a hour raise. I saw it on the TV. Martin Luther King died fah a eight cent raise? Celebrate? Dat's a damn shame!

MOORE:  They got a memorandum of agreement. That means...

JONES:  Hah! A memorandum. Dat ain't offisha recognition! What is it? A piece of paper dat say "we'll think about it later!"

MOORE:  *[Angry.]* It's an agreement made with a public employees union for the first time in the history of Memphis, in the history of the whole South! If that makes you want to wallow in pigslop, that's your choice, but, me, I'm celebrating a victory even while I mourn. Everything that's happened over these last few weeks is more important than your personal rage at a world out of everybody's control. Everything is bigger than us. It's a start, T.O.. Next year, we renegotiate, after things cool down.

JONES:  We? You mean you and Solomon and Willins and all

dem?

MOORE: You're still president of the local.

JONES: I ain't nothin', rememba? Just a bundle of personal rage.

MOORE: Lawd ha'mercy! Listen here: You need to swallow that miserable self pity. God has a plan for his people, Jones; King's death is part of that plan. All we can do is have faith and keep toiling. Faith is the only quality we have that keeps us human, that keeps us from plunging into an abyss of chaos. You lose your faith, you lost everything that keeps you human.

JONES: *[Sharply.]* Brotha Moe, I don't feel like no sermon 'long through here.

MOORE: Well, Brotha Jones, you need one! But I didn't come here to preach. Your men sent me up. Look outside.

JONES: *[Irritated.]* What fah?

MOORE: Lawd ha'mercy, just look outside!

*[JONES looks "outside" and is taken aback by what he sees. Crowd sounds emanate from the street when he appears at the "window."]*

CROWD: *[Off.]* T.O.! T.O!. T.O!. T.O.! T.O.!

*[JONES steps back from the "window." The sounds subside.]*

MOORE: They've been ordered back to work starting tonight. They want you to conduct the final vote. They want to share their triumph with you.

JONES: Triumph!? A eight-cent triumph! They don't need me for dat.

MOORE: Brotha Jones, those men said they won't move one truck, empty one garbage can or pick up one tub unless you say so. They want to hear the word from you.

*[JONES ponders this for a moment and then bursts into a rueful chuckle.]*

**JONES:** Da Mayor done tricked all of us. All these weeks of striking. All them peepas killed or hurt! All the marchin' and jailin' and beatin's! All that starvin' and prayin' and downright cryin'! King dead! Murdered! What we git in return? One piece of paper and eight bright, shiny pennies. Not even thirty pieces of silver! Eight pennies and a maybe! Ain't a damn thing change! In twenty, twenty-five years, when things cool down, the city gon' break that union. The sanitation men were sold back inta slav'ry and dey come here axin' me if it's all right.

**MOORE:** Joy? Joy is all right. Always has been. Joy is a treasure. If you can't go out there and cheer and dance and laugh and sing and cry with those men... well... if you lost your faith, then you go tell them. I'm not going to be a messenger of despair and bitterness!

*[There is a moment of silence as JONES ponders. The men outside are growing impatient as they sing or chant outside. Tears of resignation gather in JONES' eyes. MOORE silently prays. Wearily JONES goes to the "window" and shouts outside to the men.]*

**JONES:** What the hell ya'll stannin' 'round looking at me fah? Ya'll think the buzzards gon' eat up all that garbage? I'm tired of lookin' at Memphis garbage! Clean it up.

*[Cheers from the CROWD outside. JONES raises his arms in victory, manages a smile and then turns back to MOORE.]*

**JONES:** *[Sighing heavily.]* Let's go hep 'em.

*[As they exit, the BLUESMAN strolls on and plays an appropriate, uptempo blues that segues into a curtain call.]*

## DA END

**OyamO** is an associate professor of theatre at the University of Michigan in Ann Arbor. His plays have been performed at Yale Repertory Theatre; Manhattan Theatre Club; the Working Theatre (where *I Am A Man* was commissioned and originally produced); The Public Theatre; Negro Ensemble Company; Ensemble Studio Theatre; Penumbra of St. Paul, Minn.; the Kennedy Center in Washington, D.C.; the Wexner Center in Columbus, OH; Theatre of the First Amendment at George Mason University in Fairfax, VA; Eureka Theatre in San Francisco; the O'Neill National Playwrights Conference; Theatre Emory in Atlanta; National Theatre Institute in Montreal; Theatre du Horla in Avignon, France; and at numerous American universities.

He received his MFA in playwrighting from the Yale School of Drama and is a member of PEN, Dramatists Guild, New Dramatists (alumni), the Ensemble Studio Theatre, Writers Guild East, and the Black Theatre Network. Grants from the Undergraduate Research Opportunity Program, the Office of Vice President for Research and the Minority Faculty Development Fund at the University of Michigan helped OyamO complete research for *I Am A Man*. He has also been the recipient of the Guggenheim, Rockefeller, McKnight, NY State Council on the Arts and two NEA fellowships. He is currently working on two HBO projects: an episode for the *Famous Black American Anthology*, and a television adaptation of *I Am A Man*.

# BLACK HEROES
## Seven Plays
## Edited with an introduction by
## Errol Hill

Some of America's most outstanding playwrights of the last two centuries have catapulted the lives of legendary black men and women out of the history books and onto the stage. Errol Hill has collected the most resonant of these powerful examples in *Black Heroes* where we meet Nat Turner, Frederick Douglass, Harriet Tubman, Martin Luther King, Paul Robeson, Marcus Garvey and Jean Jacques Dessaline.

Here for the first time in one volume are plays—many of which have been unavailable for decades—which pronounce a Black American struggle for freedom, advancement and quality from the days of slavery to the era of civil rights. The full scope of their dramas becomes a *tableau vivante* of black history.

**EMPEROR OF HAITI** Langston Hughes
**NAT TURNER** Randolph Edmonds
**HARRIET TUBMAN** May Miller
**IN SPLENDID ERROR** William Branch
**I, MARCUS GARVEY** Edgar White
**PAUL ROBESON** Philip Hayes Dean
**ROADS OF THE MOUNTAIN TOP** Ron Milner

$12.95 •PAPER • ISBN: 1-55783-027-4

# VOICES OF COLOR:

## 50 SCENES AND MONOLOGUES
## BY AFRICAN AMERICAN PLAYWRIGHTS

### Edited and with an introduction by
### Woodie King, Jr.

Voices of Color is the first collection of scenes and monologues by African American playwrights. While scene and monologue books proliferate by and for the dominant culture, there has rarely been significant representation of the vibrant literary contributions of African American theatre artists. Until now.

This major omnibus of contemporary American writing will serve as a primary resource for African American artists in search of their own voice for the stage. Actors and directors will now have access to a much larger spectrum of work in which to shine. Readers will be introduced to a rich medley of work of the human spirit. And schools, colleges and libraries will, at last, have the book we all need to fully explore America's potential for drama.

$9.95 • paper
ISBN: 1-55783-174-2